Helion & Company Limited
Unit 8 Amherst Business Centre
Budbrooke Road
Warwick
CV34 5WE
England
Tel. 01926 499 619
Fax 0121 711 4075
Email: info@helion.co.uk
Website: www.helion.co.uk
Twitter: @helionbooks
Visit our blog http://blog.helion.co.uk/

Published by Helion & Company 2018
Designed and typeset by Farr out
    Publications, Wokingham, Berkshire
Cover designed by Paul Hewitt, Battlefield
    Design (www.battlefield-design.co.uk)
Printed by Henry Ling Limited, Dorchester,
    Dorset

Text © David François 2018
Illustrations © as individually credited
Color profiles and maps as credited © Helion
    & Company Limited 2018

ISBN 978-1-911628-21-7

British Library Cataloguing-in-Publication
    Data
A catalogue record for this book is available
    from the British Library

We always welcome receiving book
proposals from prospective authors.

CONTENTS

ABBREVIATIONS

AMPRONAC	*Asociación de Mujeres ante la Problemática Nacional* (Association of Women Confronting the National Problem)
BECAT	*Brigadas Especiales Contra Actos Terroristas* (Special Squads Against Terrorist Acts)
CIA	Central Intelligence Agency, United States
COIN	counter-insurgent or counter-insurgency
CONDECA	*Consejo de Defensa Centroamericana* (Central American Defense Council)
EDSN	*Ejercito Defensor de la Soberania Nacional*
EEBI	*Escuela Entrenamiento Básico De Infantería* (Infantry Basic Training School)
FAL	*Fusil Automatique Léger* (light automatic rifle, Belgian-designed firearm)
FAN	*Fuerza Aérea Nicaragüense* (Nicaraguan Air Force)
FAO	*Frente Amplio Opositor* (Broad Opposition Front)
FAS	*Fuerza Aérea Sandinista* (Sandinista Air Force)
FER	*Frente Estudiantil Revolucionarío* (Revolutionary Student Front)
FPN	*Frente Patriotico Nacional* (National Patriotic Front)
FSLN	*Frente Sandinista de Liberación Nacional* (Sandinista National Liberation Front)
GN	*Guardia Nacional* (National Guard)
GPP	*Guerra Popular Prolongada* (Prolonged Popular War)
JGRN	*Junta de Gobierno de Reconstrucción Nacional* (Junta of National Reconstruction)
LAAHS	Latin American Aviation History Society
MNA	*Movimiento Nueva Nicaragua* (New Nicaragua Movement)
MPS	*Milicia Popular Sandinista* (Sandinista Popular Militia)
MPU	*Movimiento Pueblo Unido* (United People's Movement)
OAS	Organization of American States
OSN	*Oficina de Seguridad Nacional* (National Security Office)
PLI	*Partido Liberal Indepediente* (Independent Liberal Party)
PLN	*Partido Liberal Nacionalista* (Liberal Nationalist Party)
PSN	*Partido socialista nicaragüense* (Nicaraguan Socialist Party)
RPG	Rocket-propelled grenade
SAC	*Servicio Anticomunista* (Anti-Communist Service)
TCU	Tactical Combat Units
UDEL	*Unión Democrática de Liberación* (Democratic Liberation Union)
UN	United Nations
UNO	*Unión Nacional Opositora* (National Opposition Union)
USMC	United States Marine Corps
US$	United States Dollar
USSR	Union of Soviet Socialist Republics (or 'Soviet Union')

INTRODUCTION

Between the mid-1970s and the early 1980s, Central America experienced a period of quick and massive revolutionary mobilisation. Within only a few years, the region, which distinguished itself for decades for its complete political opposition to change, and its dependency on the United States, became one of the most rebellious on the American continents. This confusion had its roots in Nicaragua, where on 19 July 1979, half a century of social conflict culminated in the revolutionary overthrow of the Somoza family dictatorship that had reigned over the country for 42 years. Indeed, within less than two years, between 1977 and 1979, the strongest dictatorship with the most powerful army in the region, and the support of the American superpower, collapsed against a 'handful' of 'barefoot' guerrillas and a – largely – unarmed population.

Beyond the myth of David's victory over Goliath, the Sandinista revolution was rooted in a history of violence in concordance with the country's strategic position between the north and south of the American continent and between the Atlantic and Pacific Oceans. It was also the result of a long struggle with roots long before the epic of Sandino and finally embodied in the Sandinista National Liberation Front (FSLN). The latter led a fight of nearly 20 years before achieving victory. For many years it remained an isolated and weak force, but knew how to learn from its failures and long periods of deadlock. Sandinista also took advantage of the mistakes of his opponent, the

last of the Somozas, a character whose hubris, as in Greek tragedies, finally caused defeat. Above all, the Sandinista victory fitted into one of those short windows of history where the impossible becomes suddenly possible. The general context with the success of the theology of liberation in some areas of the Catholic Church, the election of Jimmy Carter to the presidency of the United States, America's bad conscience after the Nixon years and the presence of social democratic or reformist governments in neighbouring countries came together to make possible the Sandinista victory.

Although the 1979 upheaval was part of a specific national and international political context, it was above all a military conflict in which men, equipment and strategies clashed. If in the first two domains, the Somoza dictatorship had the advantage, its COIN strategy was a fiasco, alienating the majority of the population and aggravating its international isolation without ever succeeding in defeating its opponent. The Sandinistas knew how to rediscover and put into practice an insurrectional strategy, theorized by the Communist International[1] in the 1920s, where the main battlefield was not the countryside, as for Mao Zedong or Che Guevara, but the city. According to Lenin, who represented the point that the insurrection is an art, 'Insurrection must rely upon *a revolutionary upsurge of the people*.' Insurrection must rely upon that turning-point in the history of the growing revolution when the activity of the advanced ranks of

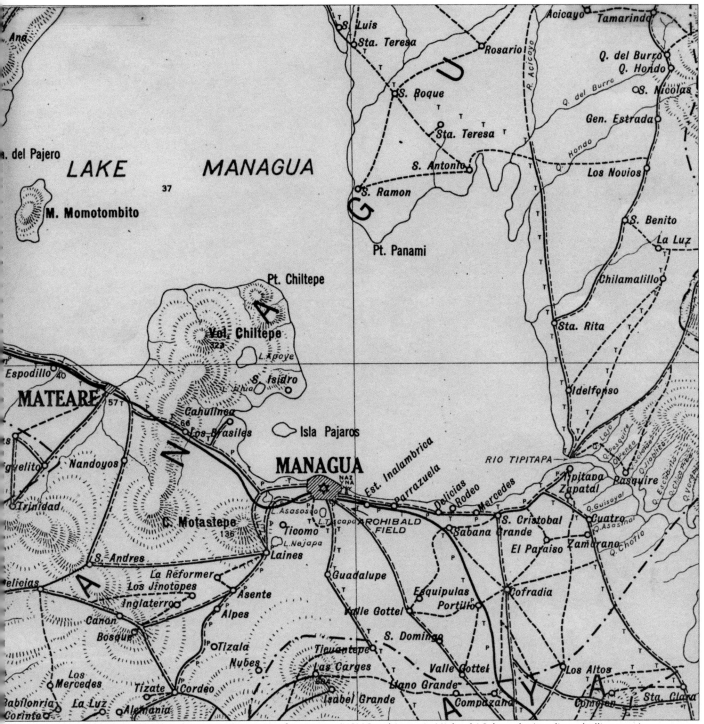

Managua region as shown on a US Army map from 1934. (USMC archives, via Michael J Schroeder/sandinorebellion.com)

the people is at its height, and when the vacillations in the ranks of the enemy and in the ranks of the weak, *half-hearted and irresolute friends of the revolution* are strongest … Once these conditions exist, however, to refuse to treat insurrection as an art is a betrayal of Marxism and a betrayal of the revolution.[2] On this point, the Sandinistas were perfect disciples of the father of the Russian Revolution.

A Country between two Oceans

Nicaragua - bordered by Honduras to the north, Costa Rica to the south, the Caribbean Sea to the east and the Pacific Ocean to the west - is the largest country in Central America. Its territory is divided into three large areas. The Pacific coast, to the west, is a long, fertile strip of land that runs from Salinas Bay on the border with Costa Rica to the Gulf of Fonseca facing El Salvador. It is bordered to the west by the

Pacific Ocean and to the east by a chain of volcanoes. The country has 58 volcanoes, many of which are active. This plain is dotted with lakes and lagoons of volcanic origin, including Lake Nicaragua, the largest in Central America, while Managua is surrounded by six freshwater lakes. This Pacific region is the most populated in the country, accounting for 65% of the population. It contains the three largest cities of the country - Managua, León and Granada - as well as the most important port area, Corinto. This region, which has developed infrastructures, is where most of the export crops such as coffee and cotton are found. It is the demographic, economic and political heart of the country.

The central region contains the mountains, that range from the Cordillera Entre Ríos at the Honduras border to the Cordilleras Isabelia and Dariense in the north-central zone and the Huapí,

Town of Matagalpa, as seen in the late 1920s. (USMC, via Michael J Schroeder/sandinorebellion.com)

Río Prinzapolka and Río Escondido. The mouths of these rivers form deltas with many marshy areas. If along the rivers the soils are fertile, this is not the case in the savannah and wet tropical forest regions. This geography explains why most of the population of the region live on the edge of rivers or on the coast. With only 10% of Nicaragua's population, the Atlantic coast is the least developed region of the country. Almost devoid of roads, the most important cities are the ports of Bluefields and Puerto Cabeza and the mining triangle of Rosita, Siuna and Bonanza.[3]

The geographical diversity of Nicaragua, marked by the contrast

A residential street in Corinto, probably along the beachfront. (USMC, via Michael J Schroeder/sandinorebellion.com)

Street scene from Managua in the 1950s. (Mark Lepko Collection)

Managua airfield, as seen in the late 1920s. (USMC, via Michael J Schroeder/sandinorebellion.com)

Main terminal of Las Mercedes International Airport, which was constructed in 1968-69. (Mark Lepko Collection)

America and Yolaina Mountains to the south-east. The mountains are the highest in the north, and the peak of Mogotón in Cordillera Entre Ríos is the highest point of the country at more than 2,100 metres. Although this region accounts for around 30% of the population, it lacks infrastructure and the few roads are often impassable during the rainy season. It is a region of pioneer fronts, where the inhabitants, living in isolation, practice subsistence agriculture.

In the east of the country, the Atlantic zone, also called Moskitia, is like a small Amazonia and represents 51% of the country's surface area. It is a region of hills covered with rainforests, between which flow sinuous rivers like the Río Coco, Río Grande de Matagalpa,

between the Pacific and Atlantic regions, is also reflected in its ethnic composition. The Atlantic area is populated by Indians of Caribbean ethnic groups, such as Miskitu, Mayangna and Ramas, but also English-speaking coloured people. The Miskitus are predominantly of the Moravian religion, which distinguishes them from the rest of the population, who are Catholic. The Pacific zone also includes some Indian communities, the most important living in Subtiava and Monimbó. The rest of the population, mainly mixed race and white, is concentrated in the Pacific region.

At the beginning of the 1960s, Nicaragua had 1.5 million inhabitants, 60% of whom lived in rural areas. Its economy was largely based on agricultural production. The export of coffee, cotton, sugar and beef was the main source of foreign exchange, accounting for almost 30% of GDP in 1960 and 64% of foreign exchange earnings in 1979. However, the country was undergoing a process of modernization and the start of industrialization. Its population continued to grow, from 1.9 million inhabitants in the early 1970s to 2.7 million in 1980, but rural population was in decline and during the 1970s the urban population became the majority; Managua had about 500,000 inhabitants in 1977. The Sandinistas took into account these demographic change to adapt their military strategy.

Brief History of Nicaragua until 1912

On 12 September 1502, on his fourth and last voyage, Columbus landed on the Caribbean coast of Nicaragua, which he took as a possession for the kingdom of Spain. But it was Gil González Davila who first explored the country in 1522-23, approaching the Pacific coast where he came into contact with a native American leader called Nicaragua or Nacarao Niqueragua. Davila also explored the north of the country, but had to turn back in the face of the hostility of the population. Heading south, he reached the Gulf of Nicoya to re-embark for Panama.[4]

In 1524, Francisco Hernandez de Cordoba founded the first two cities of the country: Granada, on the shores of Lake Nicaragua, and Santiago de los Caballeros de León, on the shores of Lake Xolotlán. Spanish rule was particularly brutal. Under the domination of Pedrarias Dávila, who ruled the territory of Nicaragua from 1528-31, the country saw its population fall sharply, the result of epidemics that decimated the Amerindians but also the exaction of the Spaniards seeking slaves for the mines of Potosi. Soon, faced with the abuses of Pedrarias Dávila, the inhabitants fled, including the Spaniards, a situation that continued with his successor Rodrigo de Contreras, who ruled the country from 1534-42. After the initial depopulation, Nicaragua became a backwater of the Spanish Empire. In this setting, Granada and León emerged as competing poles of power and prestige. The former derived its income from agriculture and trade with Spain via the San Juan River; the latter came to depend on commerce with the Spanish colonies of the Pacific coast. Both tiny outposts were subjected to frequent pirate attacks.[5]

Nicaragua, which was part of the captaincy general of Guatemala, was the main channel of communication between the Atlantic and Pacific because of its river and lake transport system. This was where the slave transports transited for Peru, Ecuador and Colombia, but also money from the Philippines and gold from China. This strategic position, an interface between the Atlantic and Pacific, also attracted the greed of the great powers. Thus the English established a protectorate in the seventeenth century on the Mosquito coast, where they founded the city of Bluefields. From 1740-86, this region was a British dependency.[6]

The events that lead to the independence of Mexico provoked much agitation in the provinces that had belonged to the Kingdom of Guatemala: under the Constitution of Cadiz, this had ceased to be a single political unity and was split into Chiapas, Guatemala (including El Salvador), Comayagua (Honduras) and the province of Nicaragua and Costa Rica. In 1821, when the Mexican separatists signed the Iguala Plan as the basis for the establishment of a Mexican Empire, the territory of Chiapas, which belonged to the Kingdom of Guatemala, adhered to the plan and was annexed to Mexico. On 15 September 1821, a meeting of the notables of the city of Guatemala was convened by the head of political affairs of the kingdom, Gabino Gainza. An agreement was reached to declare independence but to make it effective only after approval by a provincial convention. Following the integration of Chiapas into Mexico, Gabino Gainza proposed in 1822 the integration of the rest of the Kingdom of Guatemala with Mexico. On 11 October 1822, the provincial delegation of Nicaragua and Costa Rica, meeting in León, proclaimed independence from Spain and annexation to Mexico.

Once General Antonio López de Santa Anna established himself in power, in early 1823, supporters of the total independence of the Kingdom of Guatemala called for the organization of a congress of the five provinces of the kingdom. General Filisola convened the congress, in which Chiapas did not participate, confirming its definitive separation from the Kingdom of Guatemala. The congress met in the city of Guatemala and proclaimed the independence of the kingdom's provinces from both Spain and Mexico. This is how the United Provinces of Central America – composed of the union of the five provinces of Nicaragua, Guatemala, Honduras, El Salvador and Costa Rica – was born. The congress of the new state drafted a constitution proclaimed on 22 November 1824, renaming the country the Federal Republic of Central America, where the former provinces became states. In Nicaragua, it took time to consolidate the new institutions, due to the civil war caused by rivalry between the cities of Granada and León. Granada, home to the most important owners (mainly coffee and sugar producers), was the country's main conservative centre. In León, on the other hand, the artisanal and merchant middle classes predominated. The ideological rivalry between the conservative Granada and liberal León would durably mark Nicaragua's history.[7]

President Adolfo Diaz. (US State Department, via Michael J Schroeder/sandinorebellion.com)

The landing party from USS *Denver* (C-14) outside Corinto in 1912. (USN photo)

The National Palace in Managua, as seen in the late 1920s.
(USMC, via Michael J Schroeder/sandinorebellion.com)

Nicaragua's first head of state was Manuel Antonio de la Cerda, a former independence leader, who took office on 10 April 1825. His deputy, Juan Argüello, conspired and overthrew him the following year. A new civil war took place between the partisans of Cerda and those of Argüello. The latter established his capital in León, but Granada refused to recognize his authority. It was finally the federal government of the United Provinces who obtained the pacification of Nicaragua with the appointment as supreme leader of Dionisio Herrera, who remained in power between 1830-33.

Gradually, the Federal Republic of Central America broke up and on 30 April 1838, Nicaragua became an independent state. On 12 November of the same year, the first constitution was proclaimed, establishing a parliamentary regime headed by a 'supreme director' whose mandate was to last two years. But the beginnings of independence were marked by political and social chaos imposed by the rivalry between León and Granada which led to the invasion of the country by troops of El Salvador and Honduras in 1844-45.

During this period, Nicaragua became an object of greed for two great powers, Great Britain and the United States. The discovery of gold in California drew attention to the strategic position of Nicaragua for inter-oceanic traffic. Cornelius Vanderbilt created the Accessory Transit Company, which began a steamship and carriage operation between San Juan del Norte and the Pacific. British

didn't remain inactive, and on 12 August 1841, the Superintendent of Belize, accompanied by a so-called Mosquito monarch, landed at San Juan del Norte, informing the Nicaraguan authorities that this city and the rest of the Atlantic coast belonged to the Kingdom of Mosquitia, which became a British protectorate whose boundaries stretched from Cape Honduras to the mouth of the San Juan. Behind this decision was the possibility of building an inter-oceanic canal. The British occupied San Juan del Norte, which they incorporated into the Kingdom of Mosquitia and rename Greytown. To contain the British ambitions, Nicaragua opted for diplomatic channels and established talks with London involving the United States. From these discussions was born the Clayton-Bulwer Treaty, signed on 19 April 1850, in which Britain renounced its claim on a future inter-oceanic canal in Nicaragua and San Juan del Norte was declared free and neutral territory under the control of the Kingdom of Mosquitia.[8]

In 1852, supreme director Fulgencio Vega, supported by General Fruto Chamorro, set the capital of the country in Managua, in order to put an end to the rivalry between León and Granada. On 26 February 1853, Chamorro, a conservative, was elected supreme director. Under his mandate, a new Constituent Assembly drafted a new constitution, which ended the system of directors in favour of a presidential regime assumed by Chamorro from 1854. However, a new civil war broke out between the conservatives and the liberals.[9]

The liberals received support from Honduras, then in 1855 from the United States. To fight the power of Chamorro, they also called on an American mercenary, William Walker. The latter, with a troop of mercenaries, seized San Juan del Sur and Granada. In this city, he received the visit of the American ambassador, demonstrating the support of his government. Walker appointed Patricio Rivas as president of a provisional government.

Worried about US intervention in Nicaragua, the British organized a coalition of neighbouring countries to end Walker's actions. Costa Rica, which had an officer corps and an infantry trained by French instructors, decided to lead a military column into Nicaragua. Walker's troops clashed with the Costa Ricans on 20 March near the border with Nicaragua, at Hacienda Santa Rosa in Costa Rica. Walker's troops were defeated in only 15 minutes. The Costa Ricans then seized San Juan del Sur, La Virgen and Rivas. Walker's counterattack against the city of Rivas was postponed on 11 April, but a week later cholera devastated the city, forcing the Costa Ricans to return to their homeland.[10]

Walker deposed President Patricio Rivas on 20 June 1856, appointed Fermín Ferrer in his stead and then held elections in Granada and Rivas, the results of which gave him the presidency. The Walker government was immediately recognized by the United States. On 22 September, Walker enacted the establishment of slavery in Nicaragua (which was abolished in 1824) to gain support from the southern states of the United States. Finally, the American adventurer was defeated at the Battle of San Jacinto on 14 September 1856. He still resisted for a few months before fleeing in May 1857. In November he tried again to gain a foothold in Nicaragua by attacking San Juan del Norte. This attempt failed. Walker would return to Central America in 1860, this time to Honduras, where he was imprisoned and shot in Trujillo on 12 September.[11]

At the end of the conflict with Walker, the Chachagua Pact was signed between conservatives and liberals, who established a dual government with two presidents, generals Tomás Martínez and Máximo Jerez Tellería. In 1858 a third constitution was promulgated, which was in force for the next three decades, marking the most enduring period of democratic life in the history of Nicaragua.[12]

A street scene from Granada in the 1920s. (USMC, via Michael J Schroeder/sandinorebellion.com)

In 1853 the conservative Tomás Martinez was elected president. Although, according to the constitution, he didn't have the right to run for a second presidential term, he was re-elected in 1863, which led to the insurrection of liberal Maximo Jerez and conservative Fernando Chamorro. Both insurrections were defeated and Martínez ruled until 1867.

Martinez was replaced by Fernando Guzmán, whose presidency (1867-71) was marked by the continuation of political instability. A new civil war, which broke out on 25 June 1869, was resolved through American mediation. Guzmán was replaced by Vicente Quadra (1871-75), followed by Pedro Joaquin Chamorro (1875-79), Joaquin Zavala (1879-83), Adam Cardenas (1883-87), Evaristo Carazo (1887-89) and Roberto Sacasa (1889-93). This succession was finally interrupted by the uprising of the liberal José Santos Zelaya, who put an end to three decades of conservative rule in 1893.

The government of General Zelaya, which lasted from 1893-1909, corresponded to a period of development for the country. Zelaya reformed the state by enacting modern laws, codes and regulations and creating new institutions. He established free, compulsory primary education and built schools. He also made Nicaragua the most prosperous and wealthiest nation in Central America by increasing telegraph coverage and the postal service. He stimulated the construction of railways, introduced steam navigation on Lake Managua and realized important works in the ports of San Juan del Sur and San Juan del Norte. But the greatest achievement of Zelaya was in 1894, with the reintegration into Nicaragua of the territory of the Mosquito coast, which was under a British protectorate[13].

While Zelaya didn't hesitate to confront the British, he also maintained tense relations with the US, which led Washington to help his conservative opponents. In 1909 he refused to take out financial loans in New York and did not want to negotiate the construction of an inter-oceanic canal under conditions that the US wanted to impose. He then turned to other powers, contracted with Britain for a loan for £1.25 million to boost the construction of the railroad to the Atlantic and talked about a concession for an inter-oceanic canal with Japan or Germany.[14]

On 10 October 1909, a rebellion against Zelaya broke out on the eastern coast. The revolutionary movement was led by General Juan José Estrada Morales, liberal governor of the Atlantic coast, mine owner Adolfo Díaz Recinos, a military representative of the conservative landowners, Emiliano Chamorro Vargas, and the conservative general Luis Mena Vado. The rebels were supported by the United States, but the superiority of the loyal government was apparent from the beginning of the conflict.[15]

US Secretary of State Philander Chase Knox then ordered US Navy warships stationed in front of Bluefields and Paducah to support the rebels. On 14 November, loyalists surprised mercenaries (two Americans and one Frenchman) with bombs aimed at destroying government ships on the San Juan River. The Americans were executed two days later, causing anger in Washington. Knox sent a note to Zelaya condemning the actions of the Nicaraguan government and affirming his support for the rebels. On 18 December, Zelaya, who didn't want to give a pretext for a direct intervention by the United States, resigned.[16]

The National Assembly elected José Rodriguez Madriz as president, but he also failed to find favour in Washington. When Madriz sent troops to Bluefields against the rebels, US Marines landed in the city in May 1910 to support the rebels. José Madriz finally resigned on 19 August, shortly after the entry of generals Estrada and Chamorro into Managua. A new National Assembly then named General Estrada as president.

On 1 January 1911, the United States recognized Nicaragua's new government. Estrada signed the Dawson Pact with the US and called for elections to form a new Constituent Assembly that drafted a new constitution.[17] Shortly after, Estrada was forced to resign and Adolfo Díaz was appointed president. American influence continued to grow during his presidency, which placed the major state-owned enterprises in American hands.

On 29 July 1912, a new uprising broke out under the leadership of General Luis Mena Vado, a conservative, supported by General Benjamín Zeledón, a liberal. The rebels took several cities, including Granada, a conservative stronghold, and León and Masaya, liberal bastions. The Diaz government then asked for military assistance from the US, Washington responding with the landing of Marines in Puerto Corinto to besiege Granada, which was in the hands of General Mena's forces, who surrendered without resistance. The supreme commander of the rebels was now General Zeledón, who gave battle on October 4, when he was killed by conservative soldiers loyal to Diaz. To put an end to this short but bloody civil war, the US mobilized 2,500 men and eight warships. The result of this American intervention was that the Marines remained in Nicaragua until 1933.[18]

1

FROM SANDINO TO SANDINISTAS

With the Hay-Paunceforth Treaty in 1901, Great Britain recognized the loss of its influence in Central America and ceded to the US the exclusive control and protection of a possible trans-oceanic canal. In spite of the construction of the inter-oceanic canal in Panama, the geopolitical interest of the US in Nicaragua did not diminish. On the contrary, the stability of the countries located near the canal acquired a new importance, and it was therefore more important than ever to prevent the rival powers from taking control of a possible canal crossing Nicaragua. In 1913 the Bryan-Chamorro Treaty was signed, by which all rights for the construction of a future inter-oceanic canal were ceded to the US, in exchange for US$3 billion. With this treaty, the US had the right to establish a military base in the Gulf of Fonseca for a period of 99 years, and could rent the Maiz on Nicaragua's southern Atlantic coast for the same period.[19]

The US occupation (1909-33)

Between 1917 and 1926, Nicaragua was dominated by the conservative party. In the 1920 elections, Diego Manuel Chamorro was elected president and took office the following year. Chamorro died in 1923 and was replaced by his vice-president, Bartolomé Martínez. For the presidential election in October 1924, a single candidacy was negotiated between the conservatives and the liberals. The conservative Carlos Solórzano was elected as president, with vice-president the liberal Juan Bautista Sacasa.

Solórzano began his presidency in January 1925, and in August all American soldiers left Nicaraguan territory. In October 1925, Emiliano Chamorro rose against the government. To appease the rebellion and on the advice of the US government, Solórzano appointed Chamorro as head of the public force. Solórzano eventually resigned and passed on presidential powers to Senator Sebastian Uriza before they ended up in the hands of Adolfo Díaz, thus ousting Vice-President Sacasa.

In May 1926, General José María Moncada rose to support Sacasa and received the support of the Mexican government. In response the US, which supported the conservatives, sent Marines. On Christmas Eve 1926, American troops landed in Puerto Cabezas, and in early 1927 more than 5,000 American soldiers and sailors were on Nicaraguan soil, supported by 16 warships. In February 1927, the most violent fighting so far took place when 500 men of the Constitutional Liberal Army clashed with conservative troops loyal to Diaz supported by the Marines in the Battle of Chinandega.

The liberals and conservatives eventually signed a peace treaty in Espino Negra on 4 May 1927, under the auspices of Henry Stimson, former US Secretary of War and special envoy of President Coolidge. This time as a new prerequisite for political stability, Washington demanded that all armed forces in Nicaragua (including the police) be removed and replaced by a National Guard (*Guardia Nacional*, GN) initially commanded by American officers. The model of this new body was the National Guard of Haiti, also led by Americans, with the objective of overcoming the deep divisions that existed between liberals and conservatives and to persuade the opposition party that it could gain power by electoral means, without resorting to force.[20] The agreement also stipulated that Díaz would continue as president until the elections of 1928 and that the US would requisition weapons from each side while overseeing the electoral process. However, the agreement was rejected by a general of the liberal troops, Augusto Calderón Sandino.

Sandino and Nicaraguan Civil War (1926-33)

Augusto Sandino was born on 18 May 1895 in Niquinohomo. He was the illegitimate son of Gregorío Sandino, a wealthy landowner of Spanish descent, and Margarita Calderón, an indigenous servant with the Sandino family. Sandino lived with his mother until he was 9 years old, when his father took him into his own home and arranged for his education. In 1921, he left to work as a mechanic for American

GENERAL MONCADA AND HIS JEFES
July, 1927
1. Moncada. 2. Escamilla. 3. Wassmer. 4. Plato. 5. Telles.
6. Calders. 7 Sobalrano.

General Moncada (marked with number 1) and six important liberal military chiefs of the civil war, pictured in July 1927. (USMC, via Michael J Schroeder/sandinorebellion.com)

Augusto Sandino (centre, foreground) with his staff, probably in late 1927 or early 1928, somewhere along the banks of the Rio Coco. (USMC, via Michael J Schroeder/sandinorebellion.com)

The Nicaraguan Civil War of 1926-33 saw intensive involvement of the aircraft of the US Marine Corps. Indeed, only two months after Charles Lindbergh had achieved worldwide fame by completing the first solo flight across the Atlantic, five de Havilland DH-4 aircraft of the 2nd Brigade, US Marine Corps, killed more than 300 Nicaraguans assaulting the town of Ocotal, evoking a storm of protest and condemnation, especially in Latin America. This photograph shows one of the USMC's de Havilands bombing Sandinista positions outside El Chipote in 1927. (USMC via Michael J Schroeder/sandinorebellion.com)

companies in Mexico, Honduras and Guatemala. He returned to Nicaragua in 1926 at the time of the liberal revolt that followed the first withdrawal of American troops. After being unable to convince the other liberal officers to give him command of a liberal unit, he decided to form his own army composed mainly of gold miners and poor farmers.[21] To arm his troops, he recovered weapons confiscated from the liberals by the Americans in Puerto Cabezas and returned to his base in the mountains of Nueva Segovia. Sandino's forces, who lead a guerrilla war, were constantly growing. During the first half of 1927, Sandino fought conservative forces and seized Boaquillo, where his troops were at the time of the agreement of Espino Negra.[22]

Sandino refused the peace agreement imposed by the Americans. From his base in El Chipote, on the heights of Las Segovias, he said, "I do not sell myself, I do not surrender. I want a free country or death,"[23]. He took refuge in the mountains of Nueva Segovia, in northern Nicaragua, with about 30 men to lead the fight against the Americans and the liberals and conservatives who accepted the tutelage of Washington. He brought together an army of 6,000 men, peasants and miners, within the Defending Army of Nicaraguan National Sovereignty (*Ejercito Defensor de la Soberania Nacional, EDSN*).[24] On 16 July 1927, he seized the city of Ocotal held by the Marines and the GN. However, he had to evacuate the city when it was bombed by American aircraft. On 27 February 1928, he routed Marine forces in El Bramadero. There was severe repression against those accused

of supporting Sandino, with the destruction of villages and massacre of peasants, while nearly 12,000 Marines were mobilized. Sandinista troops suffered several defeats, including at San Fernando in July and Las Flores shortly after. With the arrival of autumn, Sandino undertook a successful campaign, taking Telpaneca and emerging victorious at Las Cruces, Trincheras, Varillal and Plan Grande.

For both economic and political reasons, opposition to the presence of the Marines increased in the US. The collapse of world trade with the crisis of 1929 left the Panama Canal with sufficient reserve capacity, so the need for a second canal through Nicaragua - whose right was guaranteed by the Bryan-Chamorro Treaty - was no longer so urgent. The first test of the new order introduced by the Americans with the agreement of Espino Negra was the presidential elections in 1928. The liberal party presented its war hero, General Moneada, who obtained a narrow victory against his conservative rival in a very tight election where participation was considerable. Moneada was eager to cooperate with US official circles, and the 1930

Probably the most famous photo of Sandino is this one, taken while he was underway to Mexico in June 1929, showing him with (from left to right): Rubén Artilla Gómez (Venezuelan), José de Pardes (Mexican), Sandino, Agustin Faribundo Martí (Salvadoran) and Gregorio Urbano Gilbert (Dominican). (USMC, via Michael J Schroeder/ sandinorebellion.com)

Wreckage of the first US aircraft shot down by what became Sandino's Defending Army, in July 1927 (the Defending Army was established in September that year). (*Barricada*, via Michael J Schroeder/sandinorebellion.com)

Lieutenant Colonel Frank Schilt was awarded the Medal of Honor for rescuing 18 wounded Marines and Nicaraguan National Guardsmen from Quilali in 1928. (USMC photo, via Michael J Schroeder/sandinorebellion.com)

A Fokker Trimotor cargo aircraft of the US Marines, known as a 'flying bull cart', is loaded with supplies, ammunition, mail and replacements for transportation to a forward operating base in Nicaragua in 1928. (USMC photo, via Michael J Schroeder/sandinorebellion.com)

congressional elections, also under US Marine supervision, gave the liberals a majority. In January 1931, Stimson, who became Secretary of State in the Hoover administration, announced that US forces would definitively withdraw from Nicaragua.

Stimson was now convinced that he had finally achieved political stability in Nicaragua. The US administration had observed that most liberal leaders, like the conservatives, wanted Washington's support. The exception was Sandino but Stimson was convinced that the GN, which would remain under the command of US officers after the departure of the Marines, would be able to contain Sandino.

US hatred against Sandino made him the symbol of the Latin American struggle against the power of the Gringos. If Sandino started fighting under the banner of the liberal party, his goal of national sovereignty made him the flag-bearer of anti-imperialism. This more radical position was that of the *Allianza Popular Revolucionaria Americana* (APRA),[25] which was close to Sandino.

In the eyes of APRA, Sandino's war symbolized the struggle of all Latin America for national sovereignty, independence, freedom and social equality. The Peruvian Esteban Pavletich from APRA was sent to Nueva Segovia in 1928 to join the EDSN. The Communist International and the Anti-Imperialist League of the Americas, which was founded in 1925 - not as a communist organization, but where communists played a leading role in its activities - were also close to Sandino.[26] It was through the League that Sandino developed a close personal relationship with some of the leading Latin American communists of his time, such as the Venezuelan Gustavo Machado, who visited Sandino in Las Segovias, and especially the Venezuelan Carlos Aponte and the Salvadoran Agustín Farabundo Martí. Aponte and Farabundo Martí joined the EDSN in 1928 and both became colonels.[27] If Sandino sometimes used marxist phraseology, he was not a communist. The differences between Sandino and the League increased in 1929 and caused the break in early 1930 when the Communist International began to denounce Sandino as a traitor turned liberal-bourgeois leader.[28] He lacked at that moment a political organization to rally to him a part of the population.

In 1930, despite the EDSN's military successes, and the support of the population around its bases of operations in the northern mountains, Sandino's fight met with little enthusiasm in the cities and he failed to build a political wing of the EDSN. His situation was complicated by the victory of the liberal candidate, Juan Sacasa, in the November 1932 presidential elections.

Sacasa took office on 1 January 1933, the day before the withdrawal of the last US Marines, and appointed Minister of Agriculture Sofonías Salvatierra, who was a Sandinista sympathizer. Salvatierra led the patriotic group, formed in 1932, to promote peace between Sandino and the government. Negotiations began in December 1932 and Sandino concluded a treaty in which the EDSN agreed to lay down arms in exchange for access to state lands along the Coco River, a personal guard for Sandino composed of 100 men and the commitment of the government to launch a programme of public works in the northern departments.[29]

Despite the peace agreement, clashes between the GN and former members of the EDSN continued while Sandino refused to hand over the remaining weapons available to his men. This angered the officers of the GN and when, in response to the state of emergency decreed in August by Sacasa after a series of explosions in the main arsenal of the GN, Sandino proposed to come to help the government with 600 armed men. Tensions rose sharply in early 1934 and senior officers, led by Anastasio Somoza García, chief executive of the GN, decided to secretly assassinate Sandino. When Sandino came to Managua in early 1934, he was captured and killed with many of his supporters on 21 February.[30]

The destruction of what remained of the EDSN and its agricultural cooperatives in the semi-autonomous northern provinces, when hundreds of civilian people were slaughtered, virtually erased Sandino's support for many years.[31] The history and fight of Sandino were overshadowed by the authorities for decades, but those who didn't forget the meaning of Sandino's struggle understood that the struggle against US ruling was inseparable from a complete reversal of the traditional political system and the elites that ruled it.[32]

Somoza's Rule

The withdrawal of the US Marines in January 1931 accelerated the formation of the Nicaraguan GN. The victory of Sacasa in the November 1932 presidential elections guaranteed that the job of Director General of the GN would be entrusted to a liberal. The favourite candidate was Anastasio Somoza García, who had supported the 1926 liberal revolt and served President Moneada as his personal assistant. Somoza's choice was also influenced by the support he had received from Americans since he attracted Stimson's attention as an interpreter at the 1927 peace conference. At the end of 1932, US minister Matthew Hanna and the US leader of the GN were already convinced that Somoza was the man for the situation.[33]

Somoza had no shortage of ambition and was quick to announce his intention to run for president. Sacasa responded by organizing a meeting of liberal and conservative leaders to select Leónardo Argüello as a joint candidate for the November presidential election. Somoza seemed to be submitting, but in November he resigned from his position as Director General of the GN so that his rise to power remained within the limits indicated in the constitution. The Liberal Nationalist Party (PLN) was formed to launch the candidacy of Somoza, who also had the support of a faction of the Conservative Party. Somoza won the election.[34]

The new president regained control of the 3,000-man GN and mixed the position of Director General of the GN and that of president from 1 January 1937. Somoza's support was nonetheless fragile. The traditional political elite, who had previously supported him, began to realize that his dominant position was a threat, while some GN members were not satisfied with the way the president handled military affairs. Somoza, as a skilful tactician, knew how to take steps to rally the hesitant. He initiated a style of rule based on the support of the GN, close ties with US government and co-opt domestic power contenders. He granted huge wage increases to his soldiers and began training an air force and navy.[35] To rally the traditional political elite he adopted a series of economic measures to promote it. The opposition began to collapse and Argüello, his former opponent in the presidential elections, unified the Liberal Party behind the new Nicaraguan dictator.

Encouraged by his success, Somoza persuaded Congress, at the end of 1938, to extend his presidential term for eight years until May 1947.[36] Once his power base was established, Somoza turned his attention to the Roosevelt administration and in 1939 went to Washington. He used his personal charm to win favors and maintain US support. He received assistance in training GN officers at the Nicaraguan Military Academy, loans to buy American goods, and financial support and equipment for the construction of a road that would connect the English-speaking Atlantic region with the more densely populated Pacific provinces.[37] The trip was of incalculable value to Somoza, as it confirmed that he had the support of the White House and, therefore, that it was impossible to overthrow him without risking Washington's anger.

The outbreak of the Second World War created serious problems for the Nicaraguan economy, raising fears of a revolt against Somoza. The loss of the German and European markets after 1939 was not offset by an increase in US purchases. At the same time, the suspension of constitutional guarantees and the imposition of a state of siege created unrest, but the GN firmly maintained Somoza in power. The war gave Somoza many opportunities to show his support for the Roosevelt administration without costing him much in return. Nicaragua immediately declared war on Japan, Germany and Italy, and urged the

Anastasio Somoza Garcia (front row, centre) in May 1934. (Arturo Castro-Frenzel Collection, via Michael J Schroeder/sandinorebellion.com)

Somoza Garcia, with his sons, in the 1940s. (Mark Lepko Collection)

US to build naval and air bases in the country.[38]

The rapid rise in the cost of living during the war and the growth in support for democracy around the world after the war posed a real threat to the Somoza regime, but the lack of unity among its adversaries, as well as the dictator's tactical skill, allowed the dynasty to overcome this challenge. Somoza's decision in early 1944 to run for a new term divided the Liberal Party and led to the formation of the Independent Liberal Party (PLI), which joined forces with the conservatives in organizing a strike to defeat Somoza in mid-1944. Most importantly, Washington wanted to prevent the re-election of Somoza. Despite this, the dictator did not yield until the end of 1945, when the PLI and the conservatives had already agreed that Enoc Aguado would be their presidential candidate. Somoza then invited Argüello, his opponent in 1936, to represent the Somozist cause and the latter won an easy electoral victory in May 1947.[39] However, the new president did not want to be a Somoza puppet and showed a desire to break with the past. He soon attacked Somoza's power base, including the dismissal of his son, Anastasio Somozo Debayle, from his position as commander of the 1st Battalion of the GN. The dictator was stunned, but quickly took his place by *coup d'etat*.[40]

This undemocratic action provoked a major crisis because the Truman administration refused to recognize the new regime, even after the adoption of a new constitution marked by strong anti-communism. In March 1948, Somoza invaded Costa Rica to support

President Teodoro Picado, whose government had the support of the Communist Party. The Truman administration, which wanted to eliminate communist influence in Costa Rica, persuaded Somoza to withdraw his troops in exchange for the recognition of his regime, a measure officially taken after the meeting of the Organization of American States (OAS) held in April 1948.[41] From this moment, Somoza's dictatorship would always benefit from the support of successive US administrations.

Somoza outlawed the Partido Socialista Nicaragüense (PSN)[42] and crushed the unions as he sought a compromise with the traditional elite. After a series of agreements in 1950, Somoza and the conservative Emiliano Chamorro signed a pact that guaranteed the Conservative Party a third of the seats in Congress and its representation in the government and judiciary. The objective of the pact was twofold for Somoza. It allowed him to share the benefits of economic growth with the elite and ensure his success at the 1951 presidential election.[43]

The dictator benefited from economic growth. From 1949-1970, the Nicaraguan economy grew faster than any other Latin American country (including Brazil). By the mid-1960s, real GDP per capita had reached that of the rest of Central America (with the exception of Costa Rica), increasing by 7.2% during the decade.[44] The Somoza family took the opportunity to consolidate its economic power. It owned 20% of the best lands of the country as well as controlling the trading and financial sphere of the country.[45]

Somoza also knew that his succession was assured with his two sons, Luis and Anastasio, whom he installed in circles of power.[46] The elder, Luis, who was an agricultural engineer, played a key role in helping to end the international isolation of the dictatorship in 1947-48, while Anastasio joined the GN. In 1946 Luis entered Congress and in early 1956 was already Prime Minister, and constitutionaly empowered to fill the presidency in the case of a unexpected vacancy. Meanwhile, Anastasio had risen to the rank of Deputy Chief Director of the GN.[47]

In the mid-1950s, Somoza firmly controlled the Nicaraguan state apparatus. He had foiled all attempts to overthrow him thanks to his ability to divide his opponents and his sense of compromise. To the outside world, he was a virulent anti-communist who provided bases and logistical support to American operations in the region, especially during the overthrow of Jacobo Arbenz in Guatemala in 1954.[48]

The assassination of Somoza García in September 1956 by the poet Rigoberto López Pérez came at a time when the dictatorship was firmly in power.[49] Luis Somoza became interim president, while Anastasio took the position of chief director of the GN. Luis Somoza began his presidency with fraudulent elections that took place in February 1957 and were boycotted by all the opposition with the exception of the National Conservatives.[50]

While Luis' 10-year presidency was marked by intense repression, the new president wanted to modernize Nicaragua and all the important socio-economic reforms of the post-war period were carried out during his mandate (1957-63). In the same way, the press enjoyed relative freedom, Luis Somoza was convinced that in order to preserve the system, the Somozas would have to lower their political profile. In 1959, he even had the constitution amended to prevent any

Anastasio Somoza Debayle in 1971. (Mark Lepko Collection)

Anastasio Somoza Debayle (centre) with US President Richard Nixon (left) and General Alexander Haig (one of the top advisors to Nixon in 1974). (US Department of State)

member of his family from running for president and felt confident enough to organize the victory of a man who was not part of his family, René Schick, in the presidential elections in February 1963. He was a puppet, but managed to irritate Anastasio Somoza by bringing a GN officer to justice for murder and intervening for Carlos Fonseca, the leader of the FSLN, who was exiled instead of imprisoned. The director of the GN then decided to run in the presidential elections in February 1967.[51]

The opposition wanted to take advantage of these elections to put an end to Somoza's power and joined forces in the National Opposition Union (*Unión Nacional Opositora*, UNO), which participated in the elections behind the candidacy of Dr Fernando Agüero. The scale of the UNO demonstrations convinced opposition leaders that a popular movement could be organized to overthrow the dynasty. In January 1967, a demonstration of 40,000-60,000 people took place in Managua, but the GN remained loyal to the Somoza family and dispersed the crowd, causing many casualties. As expected, Anastasio Somoza won the elections and took over the leadership of the GN. Like his father, he now controlled Nicaragua's two key institutions, while his brother's moderating influence vanished with the death of Luis in April 1967. This was the end of an era of "liberalization" and the return to a cruder and harsher dictatorship.[52]

Anastasio Somoza kept the initiative and neutralized his conservative opponents by making a deal with the opposition and giving them a minority representation in exchange for the acceptance of the hegemony of his family. On 27 March 1971, an agreement was reached, the Kupia Kumi Pact, providing for the formation of a board of directors composed of three members: Fernando Agüero and two men appointed by Somoza. This junta was to govern the country from May 1972 to December 1974, when new presidential elections would take place. The agreement provided that 60% of the seats in the Congress were for the Somozist majority and 40% for the conservative minority, regardless of the election's results.[53]

The pact split the opposition and the power remained firmly in the hands of Somoza, who remained the chief director of the GN. Somoza, who enjoyed the full support of the Nixon administration, faced only a weak and divided legal opposition to him and a tiny threat from the revolutionary left. When he left the presidency in 1972, he was persuaded of the strength of his power.[54] His re-election as president in 1974 seemed to prove it, but he soon faced an opposition emboldened by the success of the Sandinista armed struggle.

The Sandinistas 1961-74

Survivors of the 1934 massacres by the GN in Wiwilí and in the north of the country kept Sandino's memory alive.[55] Exiled Sandinistas who travelled to Honduras, Guatemala, Mexico, Costa Rica and Venezuela came into contact with new generations of Somoza's opponents, including students, who organized themselves in circles to study revolutionary theories and trained militarily. Networks were formed from Mexico crossing into Guatemala, passing through Honduras to the Nicaraguan border. Honduras was home to many groups of opponents to Somoza who enjoyed the sympathy of the government of Villeda Morales. These opponents came from various backgrounds. There were independent liberals, conservatives and even ex-servicemen, like the group commanded by Captain Alfaro who gave training in shooting to Rigoberto López Pérez, Somoza's murderer, or the former pilots of the Air Force of Nicaragua (FAN) who participated in the hijacking of an aircraft that landed in Lepaguare. Some of these exiles joined Hondurans to form guerrillas and enter Nicaragua to lead the struggle. The first attempt was that of General Ramón Raudales, which ended tragically in August 1958.[56]

The Cuban Revolution marked a turning point in the history of the Latin American left, especially in Nicaragua. In Havana, Ernesto 'Che' Guevara was in charge of supporting the efforts of Nicaraguans in organizing a guerrilla war against Somoza. Guevara faced the political conflicts that were tearing the exiles apart and finally supported Rafael Somarriba to lead a new guerrilla movement from Honduras. Cuba trained fighters, but also provided money and weapons, carried by two C47 aircraft that landed on a clandestine runway. For several months the guerrilla fighters were organized in Honduras with the support of President Villeda Morales. A column named 'Rigoberto López Pérez' had about 75 fighters under the command of Commander Somarriba, and was about to enter Nicaragua in June 1959 when it decided to spend the night in the southern part of El Chaparral at the border between the two countries. There, the guerrillas were attacked by the Honduran army, commanded by Captain Andres Espinoza, in liaison with the intelligence services of the Nicaraguan GN. The column was quickly broken and had to abandon its plans for instigating an uprising.[57]

Other armed actions nevertheless took place on Nicaraguan soil. In the summer of 1959, a guerrilla organized by Manuel Diaz Sotelo was crushed near Pueblo Nuevo, while one led by Carlos Haslam in the Matagalpa region disappeared in June, with the death of its leader. The group '15 September' led by Julio Alonso Leclaire ventured to Nicaragua in September 1960 and fought in Susucayan, San Fernando, El Jícaro and Santa Clara. Due to lack of support from the population and under pressure from the GN, the group finally withdrew to Honduras after two months. Guerrillas organized by conservatives also fought Somoza, like those of Olama, Boaco and Los Mollejones in May 1959 that arrived from Costa Rica, or that led by Indalecio Pastora and Leónel Cabezas, who seized two GN garrisons in November 1960.[58]

Due to the inability of the opposition inside Nicaragua to form a united front against the dictatorship, unrest continued developing – particularly at the universities, where underground organizations were formed, notably following a massacre of students on 23 July 1959.[59] In June 1959, a group of students formed *Juventud Patriótica*, a revolutionary organization supporting armed struggle. Shortly afterwards the group disintegrated, but some of its members founded the *Movimiento Nueva Nicaragua* (MNA) with Carlos Fonseca Amador.[60]

The MNA quickly disappeared, but some of its members formed the *Frente de Liberación Nacional* (FLN, National Liberation Front), an organization that had neither a precise programme nor any internal coherence and heterogeneous ideas. This new organization was created in Tegucigalpa on 23 July 1961 by young radical dissidents of the PSN and *Partido Conservador*.[61] For a long time, the FLN did not hold a congress or assembly, or even publicly announce its creation. Among the founders were Carlos Fonseca Amador, Tomás Borge and Silvio Mayorga, who belonged to a generation marked by the CIA's coup against Arbenz, Somoza's ability to install a patrimonial regime and the triumph of Castro in Cuba.[62]

This initial group was united by its admiration for Cuba, its desire to remain independent of a moderate ineffective opposition, the idea of the need for a revolutionary movement using armed struggle against a dictatorship and the identification with Sandino's struggle. It was only in 1962 that the FLN integrated, at the request of Fonseca, the Sandinista epithet in its name. In this way, the FSLN claimed the nationalist and anti-imperialist legacy left by Sandino, who remained very popular. It could therefore act on fertile ground and appeared as the successor, with other strategies and methods, of a struggle against imperialism and dictatorship going back nearly a century.[63]

The influence of the Cuban Revolution on the FSLN was both ideological and strategic. In ideological matters, it provided the FSLN with Marxist ideological foundations. At the level of strategy, it taught the theory of *foquismo* (focalism), the idea that a rural guerrilla supported by the peasantry could provoke the outbreak of a general insurrection to defeat a dictatorship.[64]

In 1963, FSLN leaders were convinced that they could imitate Cuban guerrillas, even though most of them had no military experience. They received the support of former Sandino soldiers, while the Cuban government agreed to give military training to some Sandinistas. The previous year, Fonseca and Colonel Santos López visited the mountains of Nicaragua to find a place to train their supporters. They chose a site near the confluence of the Coco and Bocay rivers north-west of Matagalpa, a place where peasants were particularly poor. It was an isolated region where links with the outside were difficult. The inhabitants, of whom few spoke Spanish, didn't know what the FSLN represented and were at best indifferent to its struggle. The fighters gathered in Honduras near the border with the goal of infiltrating Nicaragua in three columns, gathering about 60 men. The guerrillas quickly suffered from hunger and the hostile climate of the tropical jungle. Santos López gave the order to move close to Wiwilí to receive more help from the population.[65]

On 23 July 1963, the guerrillas seized the town of Raiti in the north of Jinotega Department. The next day they had their first fight against the GN, being harassed by its forces.[66] The guerrillas were finally forced to withdraw to Honduras. The experiment had been a failure,

Carlos Fonseca Armador, one of the founders of the FSLN. (Mark Lepko Collection)

taking place amid the general indifference of the population.[67]

From 1963-67, the FSLN organized no guerrilla activity and instead tried to collaborate with the traditional left – without achieving any useful results. On a strategic level, the movement abandoned the idea of an invasion of the country by a guerrilla force, which prevailed in the armed movements from 1956 until 1963. Carlos Fonseca Armador argued that this concept underestimated the creation of preconditions: the development of a peasant social base for the establishment of the guerrilla movement. In this sense, the work done by Rigoberto Cruz, called 'Pablo Úbeda', was fundamental. Rigoberto Cruz, a survivor of the guerrilla war in 1963, tried to organize peasants in the mountains, especially in the area of Pancasán and Fila Grande in the mountains east of Matagalpa.

While the FSLN had concentrated its activities on recruiting peasants, it didn't neglect the urban environment, even if on this ground it had to face the PSN, which rejected an armed struggle.[68] In the cities, the FSLN linked with university and high school students, who organized themselves in the *Frente Estudiantil Revolucionarío* (FER, Revolutionary Student Front), but also with the working class, especially the workers of the port of Corinto. Sandinista groups existed in several urban centres, such as León, Estelí, Chinandega, Matagalpa, Managua, Masaya and Carazo.

In 1967, the FSLN still believed in the possibilities of the *foquist* strategy. Following contact with leaders of the Guatemalan revolutionary forces in 1965 and participation in the Trincontinental Conference in Havana, it organized a new guerrilla camp in the mountains of Fila Grande and Pancasán, where Rigoberto Cruz organized networks and base support. This region in the central highlands of the country seemed favourable, with a large peasant population and ways of communication with the rest of the country. The guerrilla force, established in November 1966, was mainly aimed at organizing peasants, establishing bases and building a communication and information system in order to politically control the region and transform it into a liberation zone. Three squads of guerrillas were formed, commanded by Óscar Turcios, Tomás Borges and Silvio Mayorga.[69]

Nevertheless, the guerrillas lacked the time to train fighters and thus lacked experience, while the area of Pancasán was not conducive to the development of guerrilla warfare. The response of the Somoza

Julio Buitrago, leader of the FSLN in Managua, in 1967. (Courtesy *El 19*)

regime, however, was energetic. The authorities quickly found out about the existence of an armed movement and took action between May and August 1967. The column of guerrillas commanded by Silvio Mayorga was ambushed by the GN on 27 August and annihilated.[70] Mayorga and eight other fighters were killed, including Rigoberto Cruz.[71] The few survivors were eradicated in the course of subsequent actions. Somoza then went to the village of Jinotza, north of Pancasán, and announced: "The guerilla no longer exist. I want to announce that the National Guard exterminated them. I want to announce to the people of Nicaragua and the world that our country is at peace."[72]

The eradication of guerrillas in rural areas was accompanied by fierce repression against Sandinista militants in the cities. The clandestine urban organization of the FSLN organized many attacks against banks, mainly led by the column commanded by Julio Buitrago. On 6 August 1967, Luis Selim Shible Sandoval[73] was killed during an armed action in Managua. On 4 November 1967, Casimiro Sotelo Montenegro, a member of the FSLN leadership, was captured in Managua along with three other activists[74]. On 15 July 1969, the GN launched an assault on a house called 'Las Termópilas' in Managua. It had received reports that a guerrilla cell was located in the property. The attack was led by more than 300 soldiers. Inside the house were Sandinista activists and cadres, including Julio Buitrago, leader of the FSLN's urban resistance and a member of its national leadership. Buitrago ordered his companions to leave the house and then took refuge on the first floor, where for more than three hours he resisted the attacks of the GN. The operation was broadcast by Channel 6 Television with the aim of discrediting the FSLN. That same afternoon, the GN attacked another FSLN security house in the Santo Domingo neighbourhood.

Dozens of campaigners and city activists were murdered or taken prisoner in the late 1960s and early 1970s. The crackdown devastated the FSLN's structure. Urban networks and rural Sandinista enclaves were destroyed. Leading cadres such as Óscar Benavides, René Núñez, Germán Pomares, Julián Roque Cuadra, José Benito Escobar, Emmett Lang and Leopoldo Rivas were imprisoned, while Jaime Wheelock Román and Tita Valle had to leave the country after the execution of Lieutenant Ernesto José Abaunza. Victor Tirado left the mountain, where it was no longer possible to support the guerrillas; all structures in the north had virtually disappeared, and he entered Honduras. Borge joined Fonseca in Cuba, while Humberto Ortega Saavedra

took refuge in Costa Rica. Óscar Turcios Chavarría remained the only member of the National Directorate still at liberty in Nicaragua but in hiding.

It was in exile that the FSLN definitively adopted a doctrinal base and new structure. In 1969, the National Direction was formed, while the historical programme of the FSLN, which was defined as an anti-imperialist and revolutionary politico-military organization, was written. It set out its following objectives: the creation of a revolutionary government, the nationalization of Somoza's property and those in the hands of foreigners, the control of foreign trade, agrarian reform, education for all and the formation of a 'patriotic and popular' army[75]. The leadership of the FSLN also began to theorize about what the Sandinista revolution should be and Fonseca gave it a clearly Marxist content. This shaping of Sandinista identity and ideology was intended to allow the FSLN to acquire external support. They thus came into contact with many guerrilla organizations at a time when the majority of communists did not consider the armed struggle as a means of liberation.

Many Sandinistas came from the PSN, including Carlos Fonseca. Within the PSN, there were debates on the need to move to an armed struggle and build the armed wing of the party. If the implantation of the PSN in the cities and the countryside formed a solid base for a guerrilla, the contests were strong between the FSLN and the direction of the PSN, which always preferred electoral fights and rejected the armed option.[76] Communist militants in favour of the armed struggle were considered pro-Chinese and sent away, like Óscar Turcios, a student at Lumumba University in Moscow, who was expelled. Henry Ruiz Hernández, who also studied in the USSR, made contact with Cubans in Moscow and went to Havana in 1968, where he met FSLN leaders.

In Nicaragua, the situation for the FSLN was difficult. After the defeat of Pancasán, peasants remained in the mountains before being joined by Sandinista cadres who had come to reorganize a guerrilla movement and formed the Pablo Úbeda column in the region of El Bijao and Zinica. This guerrilla group had between 20 and 30 fighters, who favoured attacks against police stations without trying to confront the GN. It was quickly spotted by the GN, who stayed in the mountains after Pancasán, and it had to scatter to escape search-and-destroy operations. In 1973, it had only about a dozen fighters remaining.[77]

In 1970, in a very intense and repressive situation, punctuated by military skirmishes in the Zinica mountains and urban actions, the FSLN launched the slogan 'the accumulation of forces in silence'. It was a question of ceasing armed actions to concentrate on the training of the executives and the militants, and reinforcement of the organization in the political, union and military spheres. The FSLN focused its work on working with groups called intermediaries: Christians, workers, residents of poor neighbourhoods, students and intellectuals. With this policy, the FSLN wanted to bind itself to the people and detect the progressive sectors, and within these, the people most determined to fight or support the movement, notably by providing shelters for clandestine activities.

Óscar Turcios, who took over as leader of the resistance within Nicaragua, enforced this policy, which was characterized by the desire not to conduct offensive, armed actions.[78] When activists were arrested, the FSLN organized demonstrations or occupations of buildings and churches in Managua and León. This strategy nevertheless led to the release of Germán Pomares, Filemón Rivera Quintero, Doris Tijerino Haslam and others. The FSLN then devoted all its resources to training and strengthening the organization to prepare it to undertake the armed struggle against Somoza. Arms and

One of the primary reasons for continuous political and then armed unrest in Nicaragua in the 1950s and 1960s was widespread corruption and mismanagement. Major development projects – such as the construction of the Tuma River hydroelectric power-plant in the early 1960s – remained rare, fostering even more problems. (UN Multimedia)

equipment were accumulated and cadres were trained politically and militarily, some in Cuba, North Korea or with the Palestinian Fatah faction.

Despite the new FSLN strategy, the GN continued its policy of repression in the countryside and the cities, under the direction of Colonel Samuel Genie, the head of Homeland Security. On 18 September 1973, two members of the FSLN National Directorate, Óscar Turcios and Ricardo Morales Aviles, were captured and killed by the GN in the town of Nandaime. A few hours later, in the same area, Juan José Quezada Maldonado and Jonathan González Morales were also killed. After the death of Turcios, the direction of the FSLN inside Nicaragua was entrusted to Pedro Arauz Palacios.[79] In addition to repression in urban areas, the GN increased its presence in the mountains and nearby regions, destroying farmers' entire families

around El Cua, Waslala, Kuskawas San Antonio, Rio Blanco, Las Minas, Iyas, La Dalia, La Tronca, Tonalá and Rancho Grande, among others. FAN aircraft also conducted indiscriminate shelling against peasant villages. Nearly 2,000 rural people were murdered by the GN between 1975 and 1977.[80] GN tactics to eradicate guerrilla warfare not only included a scorched earth policy, but also a bid to clear the land of the people. For this, some farmers were concentrated in barracks around GN garrisons such as Waslala and Río Blanco. This was a Nicaraguan replica of the strategic villages that the Americans had established in Vietnam.

The period of 'accumulation of forces in silence' ended abruptly at the end of 1974 with a spectacular operation that allowed the FSLN to emerge from the shadows.

2
NATIONAL GUARD VERSUS FSLN FORCES

The modern military history of Nicaragua began with the American occupation. The country was emerging from a civil war that had seen partisans and private armies clash. In order to stop internal violence and conflict between Central American states, Washington urged them to sign a peace and friendship treaty in February 1923. In this treaty, each state undertook to form a National Guard modelled on that existing in the US to ensure internal peace and defend the Central American isthmus.

From then on, the Americans, eager to quickly withdraw their troops from Nicaragua, pressured the government to form a National Guard. In May 1925, Carlos Solórzano founded the *Constabularia*, a force of 270 men, organized, trained and managed by American instructors to function as urban and rural police.[81] Based in Campo de Marte and Loma de Tiscapa, it was headed by Majors Carter, Daniel Rodriguez and L.F. Schoerder. Once the formation of the

Constabularia was complete, US Marines left Nicaragua in August 1925.[82]

At this moment two different military formations coexisted in Nicaragua, the *Constabularia* and the regular army under the orders of Emiliano Chamorro. Although the former had mainly police missions, it was nevertheless responsible for training the presidential guard and controlling the capital, Managua. In 1926 these forces had to fight the liberal troops of the Constitutionalist Army that recorded a series of victories. On 6 January 1927, Marines landed from the USS *Galveston* to avoid a Liberal victory. President Coolidge also sent Henry L. Stimson to Nicaragua to impose a peace and negotiate with the head of the Constitutionalist Army, General Moncada. An agreement was signed on 4 May 1927 which planned to form a new National Guard to replace the *Constabularia*, which had only 90 men.

Somoza's forces

From 1927-33, command of the GN's training was provided by American officers, who installed a bipartisanship so that liberals and conservatives assumed command posts. Under their leadership, three divisions were formed, each of three companies, two in Nueva Segovia and one in Chinandega. The GN headquarters and air base were in Managua. In 1930 the GN had 2,000 men, with medical units, logistics and communication staff.[83] It appeared as a force capable of defending the country and the government, and from its formation it had to face the guerrillas led by Sandino.

On 1 January 1933, US Marines left Nicaragua definitively and the direction of the GN was entrusted to Brigadier General Somoza García. The government of Sacasa opened negotiations with Sandino. The latter had insisted on the dissolution of the GN, which provoked the hostility of Somoza, who arrested and executed him in 1934. After this act, the GN, which then numbered 3,000 men, easily destroyed the Sandinista forces. From then until 1956, Somoza sought to make the GN a force subject to his objectives and based on personal loyalty. He used it to push Sacasa into resignation before being elected president himself in 1936.

Somoza also used the GN to build a personal fortune, appropriating land and farms, along with profits from taxes. He associated the GN with this looting. If the dictator appropriated a share of the national taxes, GN officers did it with the provincial taxes, while the soldiers took a percentage on the fruits of contraband. Somoza thus ensured the loyalty of the GN, which increased its influence in many civil areas and controlled the rural magistrates.[84]

After the dictator visited President Roosevelt in 1937, the US administration agreed to help Nicaragua build an academy modelled on the American Military School at West Point. Somoza created the Military Academy of Nicaragua in November 1939 to train officers and non-commissioned officers. The American Army provided the first instructors of the Military Academy, and until 1948 it was led directly by officers from the US.[85] From this date, the direction of the academy was entrusted to Somoza's son, Colonel Anastasio Somoza Debayle.

In the 1950s, the GN had a paradoxical character. It was a modern, professional, well-equipped and well-trained military formation that was highly politicized and fleeced the country it was supposed to defend. In 1947 President Argüello tried to limit his influence to the military domain. This attitude earned him the hostility of soldiers who favoured loyalty to Somoza.

From 1945 the GN became an indispensable element to repress the workers' strikes that developed but also to face an opposition more and more tempted by the use of force. The uprisings led by Emiliano Chamorro and Alejandro Cardenas after the fall of Argüello, demonstrated the temptation of the armed struggle among opponents who benefited from the complicity of Costa Rica as a rear base.[86] The murder of the dictator in 1956 led to the establishment of martial law and the arrest of hundreds of opponents. In these circumstances, the GN was constantly mobilized as tensions between Nicaragua and its neighbours in Costa Rica and Honduras continued to rise.

In the context of the Cold War and the Cuban threat from 1959, Somoza didn't miss the opportunity as a champion of anti-communism to become the main ally of the US in the region. Nicaragua actively participated in the CIA's conspiracy to overthrow Jacobo Arbenz, President of Guatemala, in 1954. Somoza was also active in suppressing revolutionary attempts in Honduras and Costa Rica. The regime thus gained the support of Washington, which provided weapons, military equipment, military advisers and training for the cadres of the GN. Groups of GN officers began to study in American schools, including in Virginia and at the School of Americas in Panama.

The Nicaraguan military was thus modernized and divided into specialized units to become one of the major forces in the region. It was

The new National Guard was established with the support of US Marine Corps officers, disbanding the 'Old' *Guardia* in 1927. The Marine Corps officers involved were (as numbered on the photo), 1) Lieutenant-Colonel Rhea, 2) Captain Sage, 3) Captain Hayes, 4) Lieutenant Zea and 5) Lieutenant Cronmiller. (USMC photo, via Michael J Schroeder/sandinorebellion.com)

US Marine Lewis B Puller with Nicaraguan troops of the newly established *Guardia Nacional* (GN). (via David François)

Due to their fatigues, armament and equipment being of US origin, the troops of the National Guard in the 1960s and 1970s closely resembled those of the US Marine Corps. (Mark Lepko Collection)

during this period that the Combat Battalion and the 1st Armoured Battalion were created.[87] Their soldiers were better paid, received better training and the most modern equipment. They were responsible for suppressing revolutionary uprisings, and the Combat Battalion, named 'General Somoza', created in December 1956, formed the personal guard of the dictator. This unit had all the elements necessary for an infantry battalion, from personnel to equipment and training.[88] The Armoured Battalion had approximately 700 men, many of whom had received training in the US. The individual armament was composed of modern weapons like Garand and M16 rifles. Heavier weapons included M101 105mm guns, four M4 Sherman tanks and 24 assorted armoured cars. Recruits for these battalions were formed by a Training Company.

The Combat Battalion (the organization of which is described in Table 1 below) and the Armoured Battalion were the main beneficiaries of the equipment supplied by the US under military cooperation agreements between Washington and Managua, but also in the more global agreement for the defence of Central America. Under the aegis of Washington, the military commands of Nicaragua, Guatemala, Honduras and El Salvador were co-ordinated in January 1956 in the Central American Defense Council (*Consejo de Defensa Centroamericana*, CONDECA). The Americans also established a military base on the Atlantic coast of Nicaragua, from where, in April 1961, planes and ships left to land at the Bay of Pigs in Cuba.

In 1955, the GN command passed into the hands of Anastasio Somoza Debayle. After the death of his father in 1956, Somoza

Debayle retained the leadership of the GN, which then comprised 539 officers and 4,040 soldiers and NCOs, until 1974 when he was elected president of the Republic. At the beginning of 1975, effective command of the GN was entrusted to Major General José Rodríguez Somoza.

Table 1: Combat Battalion 'General Somoza'

Element	Manpower
HQ Company	137 troops, including command section, 1 platoon of sappers, 1 transport team, 1 communications section, 1 stewardship section, 1 armoury section, 1 rescue section, 1 scout section and 1 supply section
3 rifle companies	178 troops each, organized into 3 infantry squadrons (47 troops each) and 1 support platoon (37 troops)
1 support company	99 troops, including 1 anti-tank platoon (two squads of 15 troops) equipped with recoilless 75mm guns, 1 platoon of 81mm mortars and 1 platoon of .30 cal machine guns

The GN in the 1970s

In the early 1970s, as the opposition became more vocal and the FSLN rallied its forces, the GN emerged as a small military force. Each department of the country had only about 100 military and police officers, with only Managua having several thousand soldiers. The GN had only 4,000–5,000 men in 1978, rising to about 7,000–8,000 in 1979, according to the CIA.[89]

Managua was the home of the most important GN units, such as the Presidential Guard Battalion, the Combat Battalion and the Armoured Battalion. These units were located in the Tiscapa Hill quarter in the bunker complex built after a major earthquake in 1972.

Since the 1960s, with the US Military Assistance Program, GN soldiers had received essentially US armaments and equipment, wearing a green olive uniform (Army OG-107 and M1967 Utility Jungle Uniform). Armament included FN FAL and M16A1 automatic rifles, FN MAG and M60 machine guns and M79 grenade launchers. However, the majority of the troops – about 80% – were still armed with old Garand M1 rifles and Browning M1919 machine guns.

The Armoured Battalion, with 350 to 400 men, only had four Sherman M4A3 tanks with 105mm howitzers and 40 Chevrolet T17E1 Staghound armoured cars. These were bought from Israel after the 1956 war, but about 20 were sold to Cuban dictator General Batista in 1957. The battalion also had eight M3 half-track armoured vehicles, three Stuart M3A1 light tanks and a small Italian Fiat CV-33 Ansaldo armoured vehicle, a gift from Mussolini to Somoza before the Second World War. In 1977, therefore, the GN had only about 50 armoured vehicles dating back to the 1950s.

The Artillery Battalion was also poorly equipped, with only four 105mm howitzers, between six and eight 40mm Bofors anti-aircraft guns, a Memnic Line (*Lineas Memnic*, a maritime transport company) boat was armed with these guns to support ground infantry from the Pacific. The GN had various 60mm, 81mm and 120mm mortars, recoilless 57mm guns, .50 calibre machine guns, 37mm M3 guns and six 70mm Yarara multiple rocket launchers. An anti-aircraft battery operated US Maxson M45 Quadmount turrets on towed wheeled trailers and Israeli-supplied Hispano-Suiza HS.404 20mm automatic cannons mounted on the TCM-20 turret configuration. Usually installed on the back of cross-country vehicles, such weapon systems proved useful in the direct fire supporting role, particularly against fortified positions and to root out snipers from urban buildings.

The GN had a small naval force based in Corinto, Puerto Cabezas,

While camouflage fatigues became more widespread in the GN during the 1970s, the majority of its troops were still armed with old Garand M1 rifles. (Mark Lepko Collection)

Most of the vehicles of the single Armoured Battalion of the GN were old Chevrolet T17E1 Staghound armoured cars, about 20 of which are visible on this photograph from the early 1970s. (Pit Weinert Collection)

San Juan del Sur and El Bluff. This comprised only a few patrol boats, including older US sea and rivercraft and four Dabur-class boats provided by Israel in 1978.

The obsolescence of the equipment was the result of Somoza's distrust of the GN. This fear of his own armed forces was based on the many rebellions of officers frustrated by the contradiction between patriotism, professionalism and the respect of the law that was taught to them at the Nicaraguan Military Academy, and the practices of the GN, where favouritism prevailed over loyalty or competence. Elite units were under the orders of relatives of the dictator, the officers never commanded more than 300-400 men and were transferred regularly, and the fighting units had few arms reserves.[90] This mistrust was revealed in 1974 when the Israeli government offered Somoza Debayle a loan of $300 million to buy armoured cars, tanks, planes, cannons, grenade launchers, machine guns, mortars and Galil automatic rifles. However, Somoza only bought Galil rifles, Uzi submachine guns, helmets and other small equipment, and an Arava plane for the FAN. At the insistence of the Israelis, Somoza explained that a heavily armed GN would be dangerous and could undermine his power. The dictator did not forget that in 1947 100 GN officers had rebelled against his father to support Argüello, and in 1954 they had participated in an attempted insurrection which aimed to kill the dictator and his children.

Fuerza Aérea de Nicaragua

The first Nicaraguan military aircraft was bought in 1927 by the Diaz government. It was a biplane armed with two bombs and a synchronized machine gun. But it was not until 1936 that the *Cuerpo de Aviación de la Guardia Nacional* came into being, which – two years later – was renamed as the *Fuerza Aérea de Nicaragua* (FAN). The FAN's first aircraft were biplanes, including one Waco Model

While showing three soldiers from the GN's Armoured Battalion in front of their jeep, this photograph is also a rarity as it shows one of the Nicaraguan M3 Stuart light tanks in the background. The vehicle was apparently painted in the same dark green overall as the Staghounds and Shermans. (Pit Weinert Collection)

As well as Staghounds, one of which is visible in the foreground, the GN operated four M4A3 Sherman tanks, armed with 105mm howitzers (Pit Weinert Collection)

C and two Boeing Model 40s, later reinforced by Ford 5-AT-Bs. In 1942 some training and transport aircraft were acquired from the US, including a fleet of two WACO Model UPF-7s and a Vultee BT-13A. In the following years, the Americans added several Fairchild PT-19As, North American AT-6Cs and BT-13Bs. Additional AT-6s, one Republic P-47 Thunderbolt, a few Douglas C-47 Dakotas and two Douglas A-20G Havocs arrived in the late 1940s and early 1950s.

In 1952 an American mission proposed to reinforce the FAN with the addition of Lockheed P-38 Lightnings, North American P-51 Mustangs and further P-47 Thunderbolts. A year later, Nicaragua received several P-51s from Switzerland.

In 1954, as part of the Military Defence Assistance Program, the Eisenhower administration decided to further strengthen the FAN, particularly to protect the Panama Canal.[91] Correspondingly, the Nicaraguan air force received four ex-Puerto Rican P-47Ns, followed in 1954-55 by seven Beech C-45Fs, 26 ex-Swedish North American F-51D and TF-51D Mustangs and seven ex-USAF F-51D Mustangs, a number of Cessna 180s, 15 T-6G Texans, four Hiller Model 12Bs, two P-38 Lightnings, a handful of C-47s and DC-3s, one Bell 47H helicopter and even two Convair B-24 Liberator bombers.

However, the FAN was unable to operate all of these aircraft: despite all the equipment, it remained little more than a 'royal flying club' type of force, staffed by political hacks, playboys and a few well-trained officers and other ranks, loyal to the dictator rather than the nation, and of little combat value.[92] Unsurprisingly, as of 1956, when it came under the command of Tachito Somoza, only a handful of C-45Fs, nine Mustangs, some T-6s and several Cessnas and C-47/DC-3s were still operational. Somoza Debayle wanted to develop it into a modern service with a standardized fleet, and thus ordered a large-scale reorganization of the FAN in the early 1960s, in the course of which the remaining F-47s and F-51s were discarded. A USAF mission – also keen to turn the FAN into an effective air force – supported his requests for deliveries of Douglas B-26 Invaders. Following lengthy negotiations, a deal was finally struck, according to which Nicaragua returned its surplus Mustangs, Thunderbolts and few Beech C-45Gs in exchange for seven North American T-28 Trojans and two of the Invaders left behind in Nicaragua after the CIA's failed Cuban adventure at the Bay of Pigs. After inspecting the miscellany of B-26s in question – all of which were without any papers, and several of which were damaged during action over Cuba – the FAN selected four that were in best condition. These aircraft were then brought to Las Mercedes airport, where they entered service with the air force.

Around the same time, the FAN received its first jet fighters in the form of six Lockheed T-33s, followed by an additional example

As of the 1970s, the venerable North American T-28 formed the backbone of the FAN's training fleet. The type also saw intensive combat, usually equipped with LAU-3 launchers for unguided 68mm rockets – two of which are visible on this photograph. (Dan Hagedorn Collection via LAAHS)

The Douglas B-26 Invader was the primary strike platform of the FAN in the late 1960s. By the early 1970s, the fleet was badly worn out and in need of replacements. This photograph shows two technicians in the process of rearming the example with serial 604. Note the three additional B-26s in the left background and a T-33A in the right background. (Albert Grandolini Collection)

One of the most important reinforcements for the FAN in mid-1970 was the acquisition of a batch of about a dozen Cessna 180s. These were used for reconnaissance and liaison, but armed with single launchers for unguided 68mm rockets, and could also mark targets for faster types. (Dan Hagedorn Collection via LAAHS)

a year later, by when seven North American T-28As, three Piper PA-18s and three C-47s were also donated by Washington. Realizing that four B-26 were insufficient to maintain an effective combat force, the USAF mission to Nicaragua managed to convince higher authorities in the USA to grant permission for the acquisition of two additional B-26s and a quantity of necessary spares from private sources in 1963 and 1964. Subsequently, at least two Invaders were put through the US Military Assistance Project 'Wing Spar', run in Panama.[93]

While one of the Invaders was written off in an accident in March 1967, the remaining five were subsequently kept in a reasonably good condition and even began flying combat sorties against an early FSLN insurgency later in the Sixties. The majority of missions consisted of displays of force and aerial escorts for ground forces, but some strafing attacks and even a few strikes with napalm bombs were also executed.[94]

Four B-26s were still in service with the FAN in 1977, when a decision was taken to trade them for eight Cessna 172s: a deal was successfully concluded, but only two Invaders were exchanged. The FAN thus still had two B-26s which, although rarely serviceable, flew a few combat sorties when the war in Nicaragua reached its culmination in 1978.

Meanwhile, following extensive negotiations with Israel, Nicaragua placed an order for 14 Israel Aircraft Industries IAI-201 Arava light transports in February 1973. Although only one of these is known to have been delivered, the aircraft was equipped with Browning M2 machine guns installed in cheek-pods, and had two hardpoints for LAU-3 or similar launchers for unguided 68mm rockets. Perhaps

Probably the most potent tools for COIN (counter-insurgency) service with the FAN in the 1970s were Cessna 337 Skymasters – essentially the same aircraft as the O-2A, which saw intensive service in the Vietnam War, but also in Rhodesia/Zimbabwe and Portugal. (Pit Weinert Collection)

more importantly, Nicaragua also acquired six de Havilland Canada DHC-3 Otter light transports in 1973, and from 1975-77 the FAN's helicopter fleet was significantly reinforced through the acquisition of at least 13 Sikorsky CH-34 and S-55T helicopters: both types were to greatly increase the mobility of ground forces during the last years of the war.

By 1978, South Africa offered deliveries of Atlas Impala light strikers, while Argentina proposed a deal including FMA IA-58 Pucara counter-insurgency aircraft, but Somoza refused either type. Instead, Nicaragua acquired 10 Cessna 337/O-2 Skymasters from the USA.

In 1978, the FAN had a total of 1,500 officers and other ranks under the command of Colonel Donaldo Humberto Frixote. It was organized in four squadrons: one of fighter-bombers, one of helicopters, one of transport and one of training aircraft, most of which were based at Las Mercedes International Airport, as listed below.

The GN and COIN

Somoza was aware that his power was essentially based on the loyalty of the GN. To attach loyalty to the military, he began to distribute the running of the economy between military commanders. Correspondingly, after the catastrophic earthquake of 1972, reconstruction works were entrusted to a general. The land grabbing of Managua by the Somoza clan and the misappropriation of international aid for the benefit of the GN resulted in the passage to the opposition of parts of the national bourgeoisie who no longer

benefited from national markets because these were now reserved for relatives of the regime.[95] Added to this was the corruption of the GN in the provinces, where it ensured its protection for brothels and casinos.[96] In the face of increasing mistrust, there was further militarization of the state and other activities traditionally reserved for civilians. As opposition to the government increased, retired or active members of the military were appointed as ministers, political leaders, chiefs of customs, etc.

At the same time, whole public services were militarized; for example, National District public transport drivers had to carry out police patrols. The GN could also rely on paramilitary forces, whose members were mainly recruited from the Somoza party and served in the *Reserva Civil*, which was used to carry out surveillance and repression. The *Reserva Civil* was armed by the GN, and the granting of a favour or a job by the regime gave the obligation to vote for Somoza and to serve in the *Reserva*.[97] In 1976 these forces were estimated at 4,000 men, while the GN had 7,000 soldiers.[98] While recruitment had always been voluntary, at the beginning of 1978 the GN began to recruit by force and threat, especially in rural areas.

In 1970 the regime founded the National Police as a division of the GN. This force of 1,000-2,000 people, including women, wore uniforms and were lightly armed. They were concentrated in major cities like Managua, León, Matagalpa and Masaya. In addition to classic police missions, it was mainly used by the *Brigadas Especiales Contra Actos Terroristas* (BECAT, Special Squads Against Terrorist Acts), an urban anti-terrorism unit modelled on the US SWAT teams. Armed with Uzi SMGs, M16s, repeating rifles and sniper rifles, it was easily recognized with its M38A1 jeeps equipped with wire cutters at the front of the vehicle and painted in blue and white. BECAT units travelled by jeep in neighbourhoods, armed to the teeth. In each BECAT there were four GNs: one driving, one at his side and two guards looking back, legs hanging from the vehicle, ready to leap out. These teams were frequently used in city neighbourhoods to search for guerrilla hiding places and make arbitrary arrests with impunity. The units were often made up of civil servants and criminals.[99]

There was also a National Security Office (*Oficina de Seguridad Nacional*, OSN) within the GN, which led an Anti-Communist Service (*Servicio Anticomunista*, SAC) run by Enrique Canales. The function of the SAC was the monitoring, surveillance and annihilation of FSLN

Table 2: FAN Order of Battle, 1978		
Unit	**Equipment**	**Role**
Fighter Squadron	8 Cessna 180s & 10 Cessna 337/O-2 Skymasters, 11 T-28Ds, 7 T-33Bs, 2 B-26Bs	Attack and reconnaissance
Helicopter Squadron	10 CH-34/S-58Ts, 12 OH-6A/H-369HSs, 3 H-269A/Bs, 4 H-12Bs, 2 UH-1Hs, 1 Bell 47H	Liaison, transport and reconnaissance
Transport Squadron	13 C-47s, 8 Cessna 180s, 7 Cessna 185s, 7 Beech 18s, 6 DHC-3s, 5 CASA C.212s, 2 Aravas, 2 PA-23-250s, 1 HS.125-600B, 1 Aero Commander 680FL	Transport and liaison
Aviation Training Squadron	29 AT-6s, 10 PA-18s, 7 Cessna 172J/Ks, 6 PT-19As	Basic and advanced training

leaders through infiltration. The OSN was founded in the late 1940s with the help of FBI advisers, under the direction of Richard Van Winckle who trained the Thai secret police.[100]

In its fight against the Sandinistas, the GN was hampered by its departmental division into 16 security companies (*Compañías de Seguridad de la Guardia Nacional*) which split the troops and prevented them from mobilizing in the best possible way. This dispersion of forces pushed the commanders locally to concentrate their men in some key positions, which tended to increase their isolation, with little chance of receiving reinforcements in case of insurrection.[101] The GN had to carry out two missions, sometimes irreconcilable: serving as a police force and militarily fighting guerrillas. Either they dispersed to hold a whole territory and were then easy to defeat, or concentrated but left the guerrillas free space to function and continue to strengthen.

In order to supplant the inefficiency of the local garrisons, which were poorly equipped and easily disbanded by the guerrillas, the GN needed to create a special force that would no longer be organized territorially, so the Basic Infantry School (*Escuela Entrenamiento Básico De Infantería,* EEBI) was created in early 1977. The concern for efficiency was increased during the 1970s by the rise of the FSLN and the disappearance of the idea that the guerrillas were socially marginalized and unable to put the regime at risk, being replaced by the will to put in place a true counter-insurgency strategy. This change of strategy was implemented by the EEBI, under the command of Major Anastasio Somoza Portocarrero, son of the dictator. He represented a new generation of commanders of the GN who sought to transform it in depth to make it a high-performing COIN unit.[102]

The EEBI was charged with creating an elite corps, specialized in anti-guerrilla and repressive techniques, armed with sophisticated military equipment and receiving very good salaries. It had between 2,500-5,000 men[103] equipped with modern American or Israeli weapons such as AR or ARM Galil rifles, M16A1 assault rifles, the new FN MAG 58 machine guns and Kevlar Orlite helmets. Considered an 'army within the army', the EEBI trained its members in a virulent anti-communist ideology, exalting nationalism and loyalty to the country.[104]

During their formation, recruits were trained to disperse demonstrations and beat demonstrators, as well as to torture prisoners. Somoza Portocarrero had direct control over members of the EEBI and personally directed all its military operations. In 1978 the regime hired foreign mercenaries to serve as EEBI instructors, such as the Americans Mike Echanis and Chuck Sanders or the Vietnamese Nguyen van Nguyen.[105] In the last period of the regime, EEBI members were integrated as mobile teams in local troops to serve all over the country when all cities fell prey to fighting.[106]

At the beginning of 1979, according to Humberto Ortega, the dictatorship could count on 14,000 men, including 1,500 soldiers of the EEBI. In addition, there were armoured vehicles, artillery, the FAS and a network of informants and contingents from Honduras, El Salvador and Guatemala provided by CONDECA.[107]

As well as light strikers, other important tools for COIN work available to the GN included 13 Sikorsky CH-34 and S-55T Choctaw helicopters, which saw extensive use as troop transports – especially when rapid intervention was necessary. (Pit Weinert Collection)

The backbone of the FAN's transport fleet consisted of venerable Douglas C-47/DC-3 transports, nearly two dozen of which were acquired between the 1940s and 1960s. (Albert Grandolini Collection)

Somoza Debayle's oldest son, Anastasio Somoza Portocarrero (or the 'Little One', as he was mockingly called by the population), was in personal command of the GN, but also the EEBI from 1978. (Mark Lepko Collection)

Foreign Military Aid to Somoza

Because of its proximity to the Panama Canal, Nicaragua was always heavily dependent on support of the US Southern Command, established for the protection of the vital waterway. The main task of this Command was to manage the 14 American bases that Washington had in Central America, but also to coordinate the local armed forces to ensure the safety of the canal. To accomplish this mission, Southern Command sent advisers and instructors to the various armies of the region while Central American officers were trained in the School of the Americas in Panama. Thus, all the students of the Military Academy of Nicaragua spent a year in this school, which received more than 1,000 Nicaraguan soldiers from 1950-75.[108]

The Cuban Revolution marked a turning point in relations between the US and the Somoza regime, with American military aid continuing to grow. Between 1960 and 1976, Washington provided an annual US$20 million in aid to Nicaragua, including $3 million a year for the GN weapons and US$1 million for training. This support allowed the GN to become the most effective military force in Central America.[109] The Americans also served as an interface to supply Managua with mercenaries such as Gunter Wagner, a German-born American adviser who later travelled to Germany to recruit police advisers.[110]

From the late 1930s, Nicaragua established ties with the future Israel. In 1938, Somoza began supplying weapons to the Jewish Haganah paramilitary organization – a policy which he reinforced in 1947 at a time when the nascent Israel was in urgent need of them.[111] In turn, Israel subsequently began supplying arms to Nicaragua – in 1957 it sold 68 T17E1 Staghound armoured cars to Managua. Israeli instructors also trained the GN in COIN operations – often in Israel - and between 1970 and 1978 Israel supplied up to 98% of all the weaponry that reached the government in Nicaragua.[112]

When the Carter US administration froze military aid to Managua on 28 March 1977, arms still continued to flow via Israel, Spain and West Germany. Indeed, Israel continued selling arms, equipment and vehicles without any opposition from Washington at least until April 1978, when the White House finally began exercising pressure upon Tel Aviv. Spain also supplied equipment, including troop transports, before links were cut due to opposition protests in the Spanish parliament. The Argentinean regime was also providing weapons and intelligence to the Somoza government through its Operation Condor, in the course of which Argentinean instructors trained the EEBI too.[113] Finally, Brazil also supported the Somoza dictatorship Somoza while Guatemala and El Salvador deployed detachments of its military to fight the Sandinistas under CONDECA.[114]

The Sandinista forces

Since its foundation in the early 1960s, the FSLN was a very centralized and compartmentalized political and military organization. Its structure was very hierarchical, and all the power was concentrated within the inner circle of its leaders, the National Directorate: even all the departmental and zonal committees were directly subordinated to the same body. This organization allowed its survival in the face of repression by the regime.[115] Nevertheless, the FSLN had no more than 150 members during the 1960s and the first half of the 1970s, before increasing significantly from 1977.

The Sandinista military organization was closely linked to the strategic direction of the movement. After the defeat of Pancasán in 1967, FSLN leaders dropped the *foquist* theory[116] to adopt that of a protracted people's war. This strategy, theorized by Mao Zedong, had proved its validity in China and then in Vietnam, and was structured around three phases. The first, the so-called strategic defence, aimed at the accumulation of forces, with the organization of the guerrillas to resist repression and also of civil organizations to support the fighters. The second phase was strategic balance, when the guerrillas had achieved military success and developed liberated areas. With organized military forces, revolutionaries could move on to the third phase, that of the strategic offensive. At this moment, the rural guerrillas could encircle the cities and seize them while the enemy army collapsed.

By proclaiming the tactic of building up forces in silence, the FSLN initiated the first phase of the people's war strategy. After the Zinica fiasco in 1970, Henry Ruiz and Pedro Aráuz went to the mountains to form a guerrilla column strong enough to face the GN, with guerrilla units scattered in numerous places. It was not a question of launching military operations but organizing lines of supply, communication and information. The guerrillas also needed arming, as they then had only a few small arms. The peasants were not organized in military units, but in units of supply, information or guides.

Foquist strategy, like the people's war, placed the guerrilla organization in the mountains as the central point of the fight against Somoza. It was from the mountains that guerrilla columns, in combination with those in the cities, would be able to defeat Somoza's army. While the FSLN gave priority to the rural theatre, it never ceased to consider combative actions in the cities through urban guerrilla units. But this subordination of the urban struggle to the rural guerrilla would be at the centre of the split of the FSLN, and the overthrow of this axiom was one of the keys of the Sandinista victory.

The first form of Sandinista military organization was the guerrilla column. After the disasters of 1967-70, there was a new organizational impulse of the guerrillas in the Cordillera Isabelia around the Pablo Úbeda column, which operated under the direction of Henry Ruiz.

Arms acquisitions from Israel strongly transformed the look of GN troops during the 1970s, when Israeli-made Galil assault rifles and Kevlar helmets became the norm. (Albert Grandolini Collection)

One of four Nicaraguan M4s, showing a turret insignia in the style of a tank on a white field, with a number 4 in the centre (probably denoting the parent unit). (Albert Grandolini Collection)

Table 3: Organization and Equipment of the Urban Guerrilla, 1979[123]	
Unit	**Armament**
Column Edgard Lang	25 TCU, 50 MPS, 18 FAL, 3 grenades, 1 RPG-2, 1 HK mortar
Column Roger Deshon	40 TCU, 40 MPS, 25 rifles, 9 grenades, 1 RPG-2, 2 Thompson machine guns, 2 shotguns, 2 carbines
Column Aracelly Pérez	25 TCU, 50 MPS, 15 rifles, 5 grenades, 6 shotguns, 2 carbines, 2 MAZ rifles
Column Carlos Manuel Jarquin	20 TCU, 40 MPS, 10 rifles, 4 grenades, 2 shotguns, 2 MAZ rifles, 1 .222 sniper rifle, 1 .30-30 rifle
Column Idania Fernandez	10 TCU, 40 MPS, 20 .30-30 rifles, 5 other rifles, 2 shotguns, 1 machine gun, 1 mortar
Column Oscar Perez Cassar	28 TCU, 60 MPS, 13 rifles, 6 carbines 22, 2 shotguns, 1 machine gun, 1 .222 sniper rifle, 1 .30-30 rifle, 1 Lee Enfield rifle

Networks and contacts were gradually established. Carlos Agüero managed to organize training schools and gave shape to the military organization that was formed.[117]

From 1975, three other guerrilla columns began to be organized, which operated further north-east, between Nueva Segovia, Madriz, Estelí and Jinotega: the Bonifacio Montoya column led by Omar Cabezas in the sector of Kilambé; the General Pedro Altamirano column led by Venancio Alonso in 1975, Ismael Lanuza in 1976 and Julio Ramos in 1977-79; and the César Augusto Salinas Pinell column, which had begun in 1974 under the direction of Pinell and from 1976 was led by Cristian Pichardo. These guerrilla units were a reflection of the people's war strategy, with the strengthening of rural columns and the organization of the Sandino Road with the installation of a series of support points from Honduras to connect León to the Cordillera Isabelia.[118]

A new column was created in 1978 in Jalapa, on the initiative of José Benito Escobar, while Germán Pomares and Javier Carrión organized the Óscar Turcios column which operated in the mountains of Segovia on the road to El Zúngano, Quilalí and Wiwilí. The remains of the Pablo Úbeda column, hard hit by repression between 1975 and 1977, were reorganized in the mountainous area of the mining triangle of the Atlantic region, reaching more than 100 fighters. From there, the column, then led by Rene Vivas and David Blanco, led offensive actions from 28 May 1979, seizing the mines of Rosita and Bonanza.[119]

The split of the FSLN into three tendencies in the mid-1970s led to an expansion of the Sandinista military structures. Each faction organized its military units, especially in the cities. At the local level, units of action were formed integrating fighters in a flexible manner, mainly in a defensive spirit so that they could defend a territory both in the city and the countryside. Within the GPP (*Guerra Popular Prolongada*, Prolonged Popular War) Tendency, these units were named the Popular Action Committee (CAP), among the Proletarian Tendency were the Popular Brigades (BP) and the Tercerist Tendency formed the Popular Militia (MP). These units had to organize the population militarily, since it was not necessary to be a Sandinista to integrate into them. Armed with 22 rifles, homemade bombs and Molotov cocktails, they embarked on armed harassment and propaganda missions. During the insurrections of 1977 and 1978, the Sandinistas began to organize these units of militia, which did not have much fighting value but made it possible to support the fighting units. When FSLN forces left the cities, many militiamen accompanied them to the mountains, reinforcing the strength of the columns.

The most structured military units with combat arms were called *Comandos Revolucionarios* among the Proletarians, Combat Units in the GPP and Tactical Combat Units (TCUs) in the Tercerist Tendency.[120] They were made up of between five and 10 Sandinista militants mainly responsible for ambushes, attacks on banks and against the regime's collaborators. In urban fighting, groups 10 to 15-strong were also armed with homemade bombs that harassed the military and tried to disarm them. They were all FSLN members and showed great mobility and offensive spirit. These units, born during the fighting, were then generalized at the national level.[121] They also provided the leadership of the militias since, according to Dora María Téllez, for each TCU there were four units of militiamen who were all led by a FSLN member.[122]

Little by little, TCUs and militias were structured within urban columns. Thus in León, in 1979, the urban guerrilla had six columns, gathering 196 guerrillas trained in TCUs and 340 militiamen of the MPS, as listed in Table 3.

From 1976, the FSLN leadership set up Fronts which grouped together different military units and columns and had their own staffs to coordinate military actions in a specific geographical area. The number of these Fronts kept growing as the power of the FSLN increased, reaching its maximum in 1979. The main Fronts were:

- Northern Front Carlos Fonseca Amador, which fought mainly during the offensives against Estelí in 1978 and 1979, as well as in the Segovia mountain range. In early 1979, this Front was operating in the departments of Jinotega, Estelí, Nueva Segovia and Madriz with about 900 fighters.[124]
- North-Eastern Front Pablo Úbeda, formed in March 1978, with units from the column Pablo Úbeda operated in the north of the department of Zelaya on the Atlantic coast.
- Southern Front Benjamin Zeledón, formed in February 1978 under the control of Edén Pastora in the departments of Rivas and San Juan del Sur. In July 1979, it had about 2,500 fighters, about 60 pieces of artillery and mortars, three 14.5mm AAA guns, three 120mm mortars, dozens of heavy machine guns and RPGs. It was the most powerful of the Fronts because of its firepower.
- Front Occidental Rigoberto López Pérez, founded in May 1978 in the departments of León and Chinandega, where it played a crucial role in obstructing communications between Managua, León and northern Nicaragua.
- Central Front Camilo Ortega Saavedra, which covered the rural areas of the departments of Masaya, Carazo, Managua and Granada.
- South-Eastern Front Ulises Tapia Roa was organized in the regions of Masayo and Carazo.
- Oriental Front Carlos Roberto Huembes, created in March 1979 under the command of Luis Carríon Cruz and Bayardo Arce Castaño. It operated in the departments of Boaco, Chontales and in the sector of El Rama and Nueva Guinea in the department of Zelaya. It relied on the column Camilo José Chamorro, formed at

Table 4: Organization of the Northern Front, June-July 1979	
Unit	Commanders
Column Facundo Picado	Elías Noguera
Colum Carlos Agüero	Héctor Flores & Ramón Prudencio Serrano
Column César Augusto Salinas Pinell	Cristhian Pichardo
Column Bonifacio Montoya	Omar Cabezas
Óscar Turcios	Germán Pomares & Javier Carrión
Column Général Perdo Altamirano	Julio Ramos
Column Jorge Sinforoso Bravo	Salvador Loza & Fredman Torres
Column Filemón Rivera	Víctor Manuel Gallegos & Antenor Rosales
Column Juan Alberto Blandón	Mauricio Zelaya Úbeda
Combat Unit Crescencio Rosales	Álvaro Baltodano
Combat Unit Salvador Amador	José González

A still from a video showing two typical FSLN insurgents of the late 1970s guarding a barricade. The one to the left is wearing civilian clothes and is armed with a FN FAL assault rifle. The one to the right is in military fatigues and a bush hat ('modified' into a sort of a baseball cap), and is armed with a shotgun. (via Mark Lepko)

Outside the urban areas, FSLN combatants tended to be better armed and equipped, but still largely wore civilian clothes. There was widespread involvement of female insurgents, several of whom earned themselves commanding positions. This photograph shows Dora Maria Téllez. (via David François)

the end of 1978 near Presillas in the Zelaya department.

- Internal Front, founded in 1978, operated in the department of Managua under the command of Joaquín Cuadra Lacayo. In 1979, during the final offensive, it was led by Commander Carlos Núñez Téllez, a member of the FSLN National Directorate.

While it is difficult to evaluate the Sandinista military forces during

Although receiving some support from abroad, the FSLN was short of nearly everything – especially uniforms and personal equipment. Its insurgents therefore generally tended to wear civilian clothes – even once the movement managed to liberate several parts of the country and establish permanent training camps. This image shows a break during training in the late 1970s. (Mark Lepko Collection)

the 1970s, there is no doubt that they were still relatively small. At the beginning of 1975, the FSLN had only about 100 combatants, about 60 in the cities and 40 in the countryside. Three years later, in early 1978, FSLN fighter numbers were estimated at 200-1,000. According to Joaquín Cuadra, during the September 1978 offensive, the FSLN had 105 armed men in Managua, 70 in León, seven in Chinandega, 20 in Estelí and 80-100 in the Southern Front[125]. Following the 1978 uprising, the FSLN's strength rose from 250-400 combatants to about 2,500.[126] According to the CIA, in June 1979, the FSLN gathered between 3,000 and 4,000 fighters.[127] The insurrection of 1979 saw this figure multiplied. According to Humberto Ortega, if at the beginning of 1979 the FSLN had about 5,000 fighters, there were more than 30,000 on 20 July.[128]

External Support

Castro's seizure of power in Cuba in 1959 made the Caribbean island a refuge and base for Latin American revolutionaries, particularly Nicaraguans. From 1959, many Nicaraguan exiles found refuge in Cuba. Some were involved in the defence of the Cuban revolution against anti-Castro rebels in the Sierra Maestra, such as Bayardo Altamirano. At the time of the episode of Playa Girón in 1961, these exiles formed two squadrons of infantry integrated into the defensive perimeter of Havana and an aviation group, in which Carlos Ulloa was killed in the fighting. Many exiles also received military training in 1959 with Tomás Borges, one of the founders of the FSLN. Cubans also participated in the first guerrilla actions in Nicaragua, two joining the El Chaparral guerrilla and nine that initiated by the '15 September' group.

Cubans were not the only ones to support the Sandinistas. At the Tricontinental Conference in Havana in 1966, FSLN leaders met with representatives of the People's Republic of China. Beijing offered money to the Sandinistas to buy weapons and offered to train their fighters. The Chinese also advised the FSLN to establish guerrilla warfare in the mountains of the Pancasán region.[129] In the early 1970s, North Vietnam provided support to the FSLN with military training for several fighters, which was also done by North Korea.[130]

Cuba remained the principal supporter of the FSLN. In 1968, Nicaraguans including Henry Ruiz and Oscar Turcios received military training in Pinar del Rio. Among them, a first group went to Costa Rica in October 1968. The trip was not a direct one, the fighters leaving Havana for Europe, then from Europe travelling to South America and finally to Costa Rica. To counter the lack of weapons in Nicaragua, each fighter travelled with a weapon. Cuba ended its military training of Nicaraguans in 1969 following the hijacking of a plane from Líneas Aéreas in Nicaragua in August 1969 by Pedro Aráuz, who landed in Havana.

With no further military training in Cuba, the FSLN turned to Palestinians and the Fatah. The latter trained many fighters, some of whom would become guerrilla military cadres. In the late 1960s, Nicaraguan students in Western Europe, Moscow and Eastern Europe, including Patricio Argüello Ryan, went to France to join the FSLN and moved on for training in Lebanon.[131] They ended up in PLO and PFLP training camps with young European left-wingers. This collaboration with the Palestinians was nonetheless criticized by FSLN leader Fonseca, who blamed Fatah for its lack of military doctrine and its essentially terrorist conception of the armed struggle.[132] This criticism was particularly aimed at certain aircraft hijacking operations that the FSLN carried out during these years. In October 1970, a Sandinista commando led by Carlos Agüero hijacked a plane in which four officials of the United Fruit Company were travelling. The incident ended with the release of Fonseca, Ortega and other Sandinista prisoners, who were immediately transported to Cuba. If the links between the Palestinians and Sandinistas seemed rather sporadic, it was far from non-existent, as shown by the fate of Patricio Argüello Ryan.[133]

While Cuba still supported the FSLN, its aid remained limited in the early 1970s. Havana even sent material aid to the Somoza regime during the earthquake of 1972. From 1975, Cuba mainly mobilized its forces in Angola and then in Ethiopia. The coup against President Allende in Chile had made Havana, and also Moscow, rather pessimistic about the possibilities of a revolution in Latin America[134].

Sandinista successes in the mid-1970s again drew Castro's attention to Nicaragua,[135] with Cuba once more offering its training centres to the FSLN. César Sediles Largaespada reported that he went to Cuba in October 1978, while others went to Panama, Venezuela and Costa Rica. In Cuba, the Sandinistas were led by leaders released during the assault on the National Palace, such as Álvaro Baltodano or Tomás Borge. There were about 90 who received training lasting about six weeks, including military training in guerrilla tactics. They returned to Nicaragua in April 1979 via Panama and Honduras.

Cuban involvement in the Nicaraguan conflict was then diverted further. Following a Somoza air strike against a Costa Rican ship on 14 October 1977, a crisis erupted between the two countries. Costa Rica asked Havana to provide anti-aircraft weapons, including missiles. Cuba agreed to supply these weapons, but no missiles, and requested as a condition that some were delivered to the Sandinistas.[136] Some 58 flights were organized between Cuba and Costa Rica to deliver the weapons, mainly between April and July 1979.[137]

Until early 1979, however, there was no record of the Cuban military in Nicaragua alongside the FSLN. Things then changed when Havana established a base for its special services in Costa Rica and sent soldiers to advise the Sandinistas.[138] Among the contingents of Cuban advisers in Nicaragua were General Alejandro Ronda Marrero, head of the Cuban Special Troops department, General Martinez Gil and Colonel Antonio de La Guardia. Commander Renán Montero, who had been in Nicaragua for several months before the 1979 offensive, visiting and evaluating the various fronts, acted as Castro's eyes and ears on the ground.

The Sandinistas also received support from South American Communist parties. Henry Ruiz obtained passports in 1969 with help from the communists of Colombia and Peru. More important was the support given to the Sandinistas by José Figueres' government in Costa Rica and Omar Torrijos in Panama.[139] Following the seizure of the National Palace, Costa Rica and Panama decided to support the FSLN politically, diplomatically and militarily.[140] Costa Rica became an important backbone for the Sandinistas, who established their headquarters and bases there for incursions into Nicaragua. Mexico and Venezuela[141] also favoured the FSLN and made Somoza a target at OAS meetings.

Beyond the governments, many foreign volunteers joined the FSLN. Brazilians, Venezuelans, Bolivians, Chileans, Uruguayans, Guatemalans, Paraguayans, Colombians, Salvadorans, Mexicans and also Europeans were fighting with the Sandinistas. Some were grouped into specific formations, such as the Victoriano Lorenzo Brigade, formed by Panamanians and Hondurans of the Frente Morazánico, and the Costa Rican military brigades Mora y Cañas, Carlos Luis Fallas and Juan Santamaría. In Guanacaste, Costa Rica, the Tercerists created units at the beginning of 1979, gathering foreign volunteers such as the 'Simón Bolívar' brigade composed of Colombian Trotskyists but also Argentinians, Costa Ricans, Chileans and Mexicans[142]. The Argentinian Montoneros formed the Adriana Haidar Health Brigade, while PRT militants fought in the Southern Front.[143]

Many Chileans who fled the dictatorship of Pinochet joined the Sandinistas, usually after a visit to Cuba. A dozen Chilean volunteers fought alongside the Sandinistas from 1975. In 1979 100 socialists and communists came from Cuba, including Sergio Apablaza and Roberto Nordenflycht. Apablaza joined the Southern Front staff to lead the artillery. The first soldiers of this Chilean contingent arrived on the Southern Front in June 1979, assisting the leaders of columns, working on the staff, in the medical services, helping with instruction, repair of weapons and anti-aircraft defence.[144]

Fidel Castro talked about the constitution of an international force, formed in Cuba, to fight in Nicaragua:

> 51 leaders of the Communist Party of Chile, 20 of the Socialist Party of this country [and] eight of the Uruguayan Communist Party, formed over the years in our academies [and] military forces were integrated into this force with the prior authorization of their respective political organizations. Ten doctors and two Chilean doctors, all military, trained also in Cuba, were sent to the Southern Front to treat the wounded of the war. In an old DC-6 with four engines that can carry 14 tons, the weapons concerned were

shipped, which were landed at Liberia airport, a few kilometres from the border with Nicaragua. The Costa Rican authorities who signed the agreement were brave. The weapons assigned to Nicaraguans go to the South Front and other points of the rebellion. In one of these flights travelled the lieutenant-colonel of the special troops Alejandro Ronda Marrero, then chief of operations of this important unit, as adviser of the Southern Front.[145]

One of the insurgent-operated aircraft on a stretch of straight road used as a makeshift landing strip in the San Isidro area. (via David François)

Many other foreign volunteers had passed through Cuban military schools, including those who formed the medical brigade, equipped with surgical equipment and drugs. Each of these contingents of foreign volunteers had its own equipment and armaments, with 2 tons of armaments, artillery, anti-aircraft pieces and small arms.

The Sandinista Air Force

In 1979 several countries broke off relations with the Somoza regime and were ready to support the FSLN by providing weapons and other material resources. To supply rapidly the various Fronts, it was necessary to use air transport. Improvisation was no solution because the FSLN had no experience in this discipline. Nevertheless, the Sandinista Air Force (*Fuerza Aérea Sandinista*, FAS) was formed in the spring of 1979 through the establishment of the Squadron Carlos Ulloa. It started with small Piper Aztec planes and a twin-engine Navajo offered or lent by foreign sympathizers. Panamanian President Torrijos even provided a twin-engine Beechcraft Baron to the FSLN, which eventually paid for this aircraft.[146]

The squadron's staff began to grow through the recruitment of Nicaraguan pilots. It was joined by Modesto Rojas, who flew the Baron to Los Brasiles Airport in Nicaragua, while Armengol Lara defected from the FAN on 14 June 1979 with a Cessna 0-2 Skymaster, a military version of the Cessna 337 (known as a 'push-pull' due to its engine configuration), flying it to San José in Costa Rica, where he joined the FSLN. Subsequently, three pilots - Agustín Román Maradiaga, Manuel Porras and Octavio Ocampo – hijacked an aircraft underway from La Nica to Managua and Miami, diverted it to Costa Rica and also joined the FSLN.

FAN defectors played a central role in the consolidation of the Sandinista Air Force. This was the case with Modesto Enrique Rojas Berríos, who joined the Managua Military Academy in 1955, graduating as an infantry officer in 1959. In 1960, thanks to a specialization scholarship, he became a military pilot until his retirement from the GN in 1965, after 10 years of service, including six with the FAN. He then became a civilian pilot in aerial spraying and made contact with the FSLN, becoming a member in 1978. In 1979 he flew a Cessna 310 and carried out aerial operations to supply ammunition and weapons to various Fronts. On 17 June 1979, he delivered ammunition to the insurgents inside Managua in a twin-engine Cessna aircraft, evading detection or pursuit by the GN.[147]

One of the FAS Barons ended its days when pilot Agustin Porras was forced to make an emergency landing in the Masaya area in 1979. (courtesy *Nuevo Diario*)

The main mission of the FAS was to supply units and columns with small planes that could only carry between 600kg and 1 ton of material on each trip. During the first missions, bags of ammunition were thrown while in flight, which caused many losses. To avoid them, during the following missions, pilots landed on sections of road or improvised tracks, which was not without risk. On the return flights, the planes carried wounded fighters and FSLN leaders. The FAS tried to add combat missions to these logistical flights. The Sandinista squadron transformed a Baron into a bomber, equipped with a 20lb bomb as well as homemade bombs up to 30kg. These weapons were often defective – as shown by an unsuccessful aerial attack against the FAN base at Los Mercedes IAP. Nevertheless, on 20 June a FAS aircraft dropped nine bombs on Managua, the city already being in a state of insurrection, hitting Somoza's personal bunker. Another civilian aircraft converted into a bomber then attacked the HQ of the GN in Estelí on 16 July.

While FAS bombings were mostly militarily ineffective, they nonetheless had a psychological impact on GN soldiers, who were terrified of Sandinista planes, many of which were flown by pilots from the FAN.

It is difficult to estimate the number of aircraft used by the FAS, but no Sandinista pilot was killed despite many aircraft being lost, including while landing on improvised tracks: for example, a Queen Air hit trees along the road between Masaya and Granada. The FAS nonetheless played a decisive role in certain battles. It delivered machine guns, ammunition, mortar shells and rifles to Matagalpa that helped insurgents to seize the garrison two days later, while in León

The nascent *Fuerza Aérea Sandinista* was significantly reinforced by the defection of FAN pilot Armangal Lara Cruz in a Cessna O-2 Skymaster, serial number 320, to Costa Rica on 12 June 1979. (Tom Cooper Collection)

Another view of the same O-2, showing details on the starboard side of the front fuselage. (Pit Weinert Collection)

the unloading of a 75mm gun and 82 shells led to the capture of Fort Acosasco.[148]

3

FROM GUERRILLA WAR TO INSURRECTION

At the beginning of 1974, the Somoza regime appeared solid. He still enjoyed the support of Washington and tightly controlled the country, while Somoza Debayle was again elected President of the Republic on 1 September 1974. But less than three months after this election, the Sandinistas hit him severely, marking the beginning of the end of the dictatorship.

The first Sandinista offensive.

The FSLN decided to abandon its strategy of 'accumulation of forces in silence' in August 1974 and to launch an operation that would finance the Sandinista movement and release political prisoners. This enterprise was carefully prepared, and the members of the commando were rigorously selected. The initial plan included an attack on a foreign embassy, to take place in November 1974 during celebrations for the dictator's birthday. However, this plot was abandoned and instead the FSLN initiated an operation late on the evening of 27 December 1974.

The spearhead consisted of a group tasked with raiding the residence of the former minister of the Somoza government, José María Castillo, in Los Robles outside Managua. This operation was organized by Pedro Arauz, under the control of Tomás Borge.[149] That evening, the house was hosting a reception in honour of the US ambassador, who had the judicious idea to leave the party half an hour before the intrusion of 12 guerrillas of the commando Juan José Quezada, under the orders of Eduardo Contreras Escobar. The commando had a diverse arsenal: a shotgun, a pistol, a .22 rifle, an AR15 and an M1 rifle, and an M3 submachine gun. Once on the site, the insurgents came under fire from a sergeant of the OSN but managed to enter the house and bring it under their control. The owner, José María Castillo, was shot dead during the quick exchange of fire while trying to look for a weapon to defend himself.[150]

The commando captured many leading personalities, including Somoza's brother-in-law, the Minister of Foreign Affairs, the mayor of Managua, the head of Esso in Nicaragua and the ambassador of Chile. The Sandinistas made known their demands to set the hostages free, including the release of political prisoners such as Daniel Ortega

Saavedra, a ransom of $5 million and the publication of a FSLN communiqué in the newspapers. Somoza reacted by decreeing a state of siege, arresting many political opponents and reinforcing the police with GN troops. Castillo's house was surrounded by military patrols.[151]

Negotiations began under the mediation of Monsignor Miguel Obando y Bravo, the Bishop of Managua. After managing to reduce the ransom to about $1 million, Somoza bowed to the Sandinista demands. On 30 December, the 13 guerrillas and 14 former political prisoners boarded a plane to Cuba while the hostages were released. The FSLN operation cost the lives of four people; three others – including one insurgent – were injured.[152]

In the countryside, after leading actions in 1974 against local administrators, FSLN guerrillas also went on the offensive. The column Pablo Úbeda, led by Carlos Agüero, attacked the GN garrison at Waslala. In the Matagalpa area, where the column headed by Victor Tirado López was located, the Sandinista combat unit Luisa Amanda Espinoza, led by Edgard Munguia and including about 40 men, captured the small town of Río Blanco on 21 March 1975.[153] They were quickly expelled by the GN, suffering significant losses for no gain. Nevertheless, the insurgents then organized an ambush against a convoy of the GN that was totally destroyed at Kuskawás on 9 September.

However, these actions were too few, failing to arouse any echo in the cities, where repressions were strong, while an ambush at Kuskawás provoked a disagreement between Victor Tirado and Henry Ruiz concerning the tactics to be followed in the mountains.

Humiliated by the Sandinista raid on the Castillo house, Somoza unleashed the GN in a fierce counter-insurgency campaign throughout the territory. The BECAT dismantled cells of the FSLN in the cities, while in rural areas the Combat Battalion delivered multiple severe blows: in 1975 the regime launched a military offensive against the column Pablo Úbeda in the north of the country; in August 1976 there followed Operation Aguila VI, which involved troops from Guatemala, El Salvador and a contingent of US military officers that directed all the operations. Forces of the GN destroyed many guerrilla groups, mostly in northern Nicaragua. Meanwhile, in August 1975, the GN

A typical 'search and destroy' operation by the GN in the mid-1970s included daily raids of even the smallest villages and farms in the search for insurgents. Thousands of civilians were tortured in the process and many suspects summarily executed. (Mark Lepko Collection)

also assaulted a FSLN training base in El Sauce, north of Managua: four insurgents were killed and the base completely destroyed. Near the border with Honduras, the GN attacked guerrillas in Ocotal, while in the province of Carazo soldiers raided the towns of Chinandega and Jinotepe, both of which were renowned as strongholds of the insurgency.[154] Overall, up to 3,000 people were killed by the military in the Nicaraguan countryside between 1974 and 1977, while even more went missing.[155]

November 1976 was a deadly month for the FSLN. On 7 November, Eduardo Contreras, commander of the 1974 Christmas operation, was shot dead with two other guerrillas in Managua by a BECAT patrol.[156] Carlos Roberto Huembes was killed the same day. After leaving Francisco Rivera Quintero, known as 'El Zorro', near the Iyas River, Carlos Fonseca, the main leader of the FSLN, and two other guerrillas were tracked down in the mountains of the Zinica region and ambushed in Boca de Piedra. One of the guerrillas died immediately, while Fonseca was seriously wounded in the right leg and died at dawn the next day.[157]. The soldiers cut off his head and hands, which they took back to Managua as proof of this death and to demonstrate the strength of the regime. However, this only succeeded in making Fonseca a martyr and a hero.

The Somozist offensive against the guerrillas did not spare the civilian population. In the mountains, the GN did not hesitate to destroy villages and kill livestock to quell the guerrillas by removing any opportunity to resupply. The military felt it was at war against a part of the population described as 'terrorists' and 'communists', which first triggered persecutions against the peasants and then campaigns of terror. In January 1975, a campaign began in the northern zone of the country, and the GN multiplied its abuses in the departments of Matagalpa, Nueva Segovia, Jinotega and Zelaya, burning farms and bombarding the inhabitants. During these operations, the men of a village were taken and 20 of them were shot. The GN burst into mountainous areas by helicopter, accusing the peasants of holding weapons or supplying guerrillas. Many were arrested, locked up, tortured or murdered, while others simply disappeared. In El Naranjo, eight women were raped by the GN,[158] which also opened concentration camps in the regions of Kilala, Chinandega, Amatillo, Ococona, Rio Blanco and Waslala. They imprisoned not only the captured peasants but also the populations of whole areas which refused to submit.[159]

Under the severe blows of the dictatorship, FSLN fighters had to retreat to seek refuge in the most remote areas of the country. The repression especially prevented the Sandinistas from structuring their columns and forced them to remain on the defensive until the autumn of 1977. The situation was not so desperate for the Sandinistas, however, since the regime's offensives did not destroy the guerrillas who, on the contrary, received greater support from the population. The Sandinistas managed to develop urban guerrilla nuclei and launched some offensive actions in late 1976. At the end of September they attacked the GN garrison in Masaya, also launching actions in the cities of León and Estelí.[160] While in the summer of 1977 the FSLN claimed the death of 37 GN soldiers during ambushes, these actions were mainly in the Cordillera Isabela, a mountainous area favourable to the guerrillas but away from the nerve centres of the country. Politically, the FSLN was still not seen as a central player in the opposition to Somoza, and even less as a plausible alternative to the dictatorship.

The decision to go on the offensive in 1974 therefore appeared to be an error for the FSLN. The goal of reinforcing the guerrillas was not achieved, while Somoza managed to take the initiative by launching a campaign of censorship of the press, proclaiming a state of siege and martial law and setting up military tribunals.

The December 1974 hostage-taking operation, however, showed the effectiveness of the FSLN and the fragility of the dictatorship. The repressions negatively affected the image of the regime, both with the Nicaraguan bourgeoisie and international opinion, including the

US. It also forced the civil opposition to take a more radical stance, since for more than two-and-a-half years political freedom, already well reduced, had become practically non-existent. All this led in the following years to a rapprochement between the civil opposition and the Sandinistas.

Split in the FSLN

On the military side, the 1974-75 offensive was a failure for the Sandinistas. Since its birth, the FSLN's strategy had relied exclusively on the mountains, on guerrilla groups which, linked to the peasantry, struck the GN in order to trigger an insurrection. All the best cadres and elements were sent to the mountains. Work in the cities, whether for recruiting or looking for supplies to be sent to the guerrillas, revolved around the mountains. This strategy was not called into question, and in the north of the country Bayardo Arce formed combat units in rural areas and organized the Sandino Road, which was to connect cities to the mountains through the countryside. The establishment of guerrilla units in the intermediate zones provided supplies and fighters, as the Ho Chi Minh Trail had done in Vietnam. But the gradual smothering of the guerrillas forced them onto the defensive and suppressed the tactical initiative, rapidly causing a crisis inside the FSLN.[161]

From 1975 a discussion arose within the Sandinista leadership about tactics and revolutionary strategy. The majority remained faithful to the guerrilla strategy and considered that the mountains remained the political axis and the central military theatre. It had rejected the *foquist* strategy for adopting a people's war with a long struggle, based on the peasantry, on the model of the Chinese revolution and the Vietnamese struggle.[162] It gathered in a protracted people's war tendency, while a minority favoured a proletarian tendency, led by Jaime Wheelock,[163] with a strategy based on the support of workers or semi-proletarians in urban areas. The proletarians defended an orthodox Marxist vision that made the working class - urban and rural - the vanguard of the struggle.[164] This tendency denounced the romantic and petty-bourgeois character of guerrilla supporters in the mountains. Wheelock and his supporters were excluded from the FSLN in October 1975 and formed an organization that continued its action in the cotton-growing area in the north-west of the country.

A new split occurred in early 1977 when Humberto Ortega tried to persuade the FSLN leadership that conditions for an insurrectional civil war were already present in Nicaragua. The proponents of this thesis were structured in a tendency called *Insurreccional* or *Tercerista*, which differed from previous ones on the question of the rhythm of the revolution. To the GPP or proletarians, the level of revolutionary consciousness of the people was low and therefore needed to be developed through education and struggle. These two tendencies were part of a long-term military struggle. For the Tercerists, this level of consciousness would never reach a higher revolutionary stage, which meant that they had to take action quickly while society had experienced a rapid radicalization and the central power was weakened.[165]

The mass movement appeared to the Tercerists as the central axis of the insurrectional process at a time when the FSLN was increasing its activity among marginalized urban groups, the progressive middle class and even in certain circles of high society. For them, the city was at the heart of the military and political struggle. They therefore advocated a search for alliances with the bourgeoisie, and for this reason established a programme that was based on political pluralism, a mixed economy and non-alignment in the international field. The Tercerists thus shifted the centre of gravity of the struggle towards the urban areas in a situation where society was politicized quickly. A policy of alliance with the bourgeoisie opposed to Somoza was necessary to allow support from parts of Nicaraguan society with a pluralist opinion, international social democracy and especially foreign public opinion and states.[166]

In attempt to put an end to the rift among the Sandinistas, Carlos Fonseca returned to Nicaragua – illegally – in March 1976. He settled in the mountains in order to gather the principal leaders to solve the contradictions within the organization and reunify the FSLN. While he favoured the idea of a 'people's war', he also wanted the movement to carry out political work in the cities.[167] His death in November prevented him from achieving his goal. Thus, the Sandinistas eventually launched their final assault on the Somoza regime while still split into three ideologically separate factions.

Guerrilla crisis

The early 1970s marked a turning point in the history of Nicaragua. If the FSLN remained a marginal organization, the pact signed between Somoza and the leader of the conservatives, Agüero, put an end to the hopes of the moderate opposition to establish reforms by the regime. The earthquake that destroyed Managua on 23 December 1972 was an opportunity for Somoza and the GN to get their hands on the national economy, evading the traditional economic circles that until then

Like the earthquake and subsequent fire of 31 March 1931, which virtually destroyed old Managua, the earthquake of 23 December 1972 once again ruined the second largest city of Central America. The Nicaraguan capital took decades to recover, and most of the population has since been living in newly built residential areas well away from the city centre – in turn making control over civilians an increasingly problematic issue for the authorities. (Mark Lepko Collection)

had been loyal to the regime but were gradually moving towards the opposition.[168] The bourgeoisie also lost confidence in the dictatorship's ability to ensure adequate conditions for the country's development, thereby broadening the social base that opposed the dictatorship. The escalation of the economic crisis and rising discontent finally triggered a political crisis: even the middle and upper classes – which until then had adapted their interests to the conditions imposed by the dictatorship – began leaning towards the opposition.

These forces were grouped together in the Union of Democratic Liberation (*Unión Democrática de Liberación*, UDEL), founded and led by Pedro Joaquín Chamorro and a group of activists of the Conservative Party. The UDEL, which included members of conservative parties, social-Christians, socialists and trade union representatives opposed to Somoza, called for abstention in the presidential elections of 1974 and for a national dialogue with the regime on the basis of minimum demands published in *La Prensa*: the application of political and trade union freedoms, the ending of censorship and state of siege, the cessation of repression, amnesty for political prisoners and the return of exiles.[169] The UDEL quickly became the dominant anti-Somoza organization in the discontented sectors of the bourgeoisie.[170]

In mid-1977, this bourgeois opposition was in great turmoil, encouraged by the new Carter administration's shift of US foreign policy. Refusing the defence of the status quo in Central America, Jimmy Carter decided to link US support for Latin American regimes to respect for human rights.[171] On 28 March 1977, worried about the repressive policy of the Somoza regime, American military aid of $2.5 million in Nicaragua was suspended following a report by the US Congress on the GN's actions.[172] This policy rapidly produced an effect. On 19 September, martial law was lifted and Somoza called municipal elections. This gesture finally allowed him to receive military aid again from Washington.[173] If Somoza agreed and responded favourably to American demands, it was because he was convinced that he had managed to annihilate the FSLN – or at least reduced the movement to a bare minimum.

Indeed, at a time when the insurgency was divided into three factions, its armed groups were suffering from almost total isolation, and a lack of supplies and information, which prevented them from influencing the debate on the line to follow. The GN, which cut ties with Managua and Jinotega, decimated the guerrillas little by little, while the combatants were also victims of malaria and leprosy in the mountains.[174] All this forced the guerrilla groups to move deeper into the mountains, to separate from their peasant social base and suffer the rigours of isolation, the loss of contact with other units and the Sandinista organization, in the mountains, cities and abroad.

The situation of the main guerrilla column, Pablo Úbeda, became critical when the GN managed to reach its main camp on 9 December 1976. The camp was moved, but two months later, on 9 February, was attacked again. To restore some life to the column, in March its command decided to create the column Aurelio Carrasco, an elite troop responsible for offensive missions, while the rest of the column remained in the mountains. The column Carrasco was led by Carlos Agüero, who was killed in its first mission on 7 April. The death of Agüero, added to that of Carlos Fonseca, Eduardo Contreras, Edgar Munguía and Filemón Rivera, meant that almost the entire FSLN leadership had disappeared.[175]

During the rest of the year, the GN's encirclement of the Carrasco column was tightened. The column suffered from hunger and isolation, becoming demoralized. In July, part of the group tried to break the encirclement to reach the city, but its members were killed, wounded or taken prisoner. The other part of the column decided to leave the mountains to head for Honduras. It reached the Patuca River on 31 December 1977.

Almost at the same time as column Aurelio Carrasco was disbanded, column Pablo Úbeda, which also included the elderly, women and children, decided to split in two: some went to the forests of Saslaya under the direction of David Blanco, while others, under the orders of René Vivas and Serafín García, travelled to Kilambe and El Naranjo.[176]

Blanco's group was detected and attacked by the GN, but managed to establish contact with Bayardo Arce and reinforced the column Bonifacio Montoya. Henry Ruiz managed to make contact with René Vivas' group, and tried to rebuild the column Úbeda. The other groups that gravitated around this column were disintegrating. That led by Victor Tirado was the victim of brutal repression by the GN and lost its social base. It was landlocked in the San Antonio area of Kuskawás and Pancasán, with only five fighters. Tirado eventually reconnected with Camilo Ortega and joined the Tercerist Tendency. For its part, the unit of Francisco Rivera had only six fighters.[177]

The October 1977 Offensive

It was at this moment, when the guerrillas had suffered rough blows and had often disappeared, that the Tercerists decided to launch an offensive. This decision was based on political, strategic and military considerations. At the political level, it was a question of taking the political and military initiative to prevent the American government setting up 'Somozism without Somoza'. On this point, the Sandinistas understood the intentions of the Carter administration in seeking an alternative to Somoza, relying on the UDEL to isolate the FSLN, whose position was considered too radical or socialist by Washington. The Sandinistas had to regain control of their position in the centre of the political game, but without losing it as it did after 27 December 1974. The development of offensive actions was also vital to increase confidence in victory, among both the population and the FSLN's national and international allies. The support of international public opinion required visible and spectacular actions.

However, part of the international community, as well as the bourgeois opposition to Somoza, were wary of the ideological orientation of the guerrilla forces. Somoza had described the Sandinista movement as a communist one, and the official statements of the FSLN had a Marxist connotation that could scare the bourgeoisie. The Tercerist leadership therefore considered it important to change the FSLN's image, with the incorporation into its ranks of conservative anti-Somozist figures like Edén Pastora.

The offensive planned by the Tercerists also aimed to impose their military conceptions on the conduct of the fight against Somoza. In May 1977, the Tercerists developed a strategy of insurrectional character that relied on both guerrilla warfare and urban armed struggle, with insurgency as a central axis.[178] If the Sandinista strategy had hitherto considered the population as a guerrilla support, so that the latter as such could defeat the GN, for the Tercerists the guerrillas had to instead support the population so that it, through insurrection, could beat their opponents. The Tercerists therefore believed that it was necessary to activate not only the guerrilla forces but also the population to participate actively in the armed struggle. In this way, the FSLN had to maintain a situation of total mobilization - social, economic and political - to make possible the dispersal of the military capacities of the GN.[179]

Tercerists began to take action during the course of 1977 by infiltrating fighters in the departments of Nueva Segovia, Estelí, Matagalpa and Jinotega. The offensive operation code named *Ródrigo is not Dead* was launched on 4 May 1977 in Managua and Estelí,

The oldest type still in service with the FAN in the 1970s were survivors from a batch of seven Beech 18s (a civilian variant of the C-45 Expeditor), acquired in 1956. Very little is known about their looks at this time, except that they seem to have had their rooves painted in white, while the rest of the fuselage and wings were left in bare metal. The service title was applied on the upper fuselage, in the same dark blue colour as the cheat line and stripes on the fins. It remains unclear if they still had any roundels on the top or bottom surfaces of the wings. (Artwork by Tom Cooper)

Between 1948 and 1963, the FAN acquired a total of 13 Douglas C-47s (or their civilian variant, DC-3s), and the type underwent intensive service, resulting in only a handful remaining operational by 1979. As far as is known, the livery of all examples was essentially the same: top surfaces and the sides of the fuselage and fin were painted in white, with undersurfaces of the fuselage, as well as the entire wing, either in silver-grey (early on) or mid-grey (1960s and 1970s). A relatively thin blue cheat line separated the two basic colours. Known serials were in the range 410-418. Inset is the actual FAN roundel, consisting of a white triangle on a blue field, which was outlined in red. Depending on the period in question, this was applied either on both top and bottom surfaces of the wing, or only on the top surface of the left and bottom surface of the right wing. (Artwork by Tom Cooper)

In 1977, the FAN acquired one Piper PA-23-250 Aztec light transport. As far as is known, the aircraft seems to have been painted in the same light blue-grey overall, like surviving T-33Bs around the same time. It also received a big anti-glare panel applied in front of the cockpit and the serial 1018. It remains unknown if it received any other national insignia except the usual red and blue stripes on the fin. The sole Aztec was accompanied by one Beech A-35 Bonanza, acquired in 1975 and serialed 1017. (Artwork by Tom Cooper)

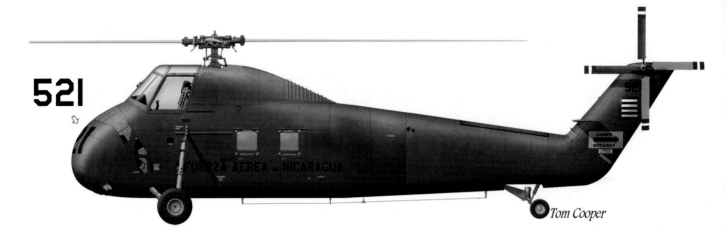

Starting in 1975, the FAN was donated a total of 10 Sikorsky CH-34A and S-58T Choctaw helicopters. Serialed in the range 517-527, these were operated by the *Escuadrón de Ala Rotatoria*, which is known to have lost at least three of its machines in combat or accidents (the serial 517 on 7 September 1976 and serial 519 and 523 on 17 November 1978). This example might have been written off too, because an S-58T is known to have worn the same serial in 1978. CH-34As were originally left in the same livery as delivered, in the so-called 'US Army Helicopter Drab' (FS34031) overall, as shown here. Service titles were applied on the side of the cabin, while serials were worn on the nose and near the top of the fin. (Artwork by Tom Cooper)

In 1977, the Nicaraguan fleet of CH-34As was reinforced through the addition of three Choctaws, serials 525 (55-4504), 526 (54-3019) and 527 (55-4488). At least the first two of these were painted in light blue-grey overall, and received slightly different service titles, partially applied on the boom. Note the fin flash adopted in the 1977-78 period, including only three blue and two white stripes. (Artwork by Tom Cooper)

Nicaragua received at least three S-55Ts, including 57-1699, 57-1750 and 56-4313. These reportedly received FAN serials 520-522, although visual evidence confirms another with the serial number 519. All three were painted in the same or similar colours used for the famous 'South East Asia' camouflage pattern in the USA, including light brown, green (FS34102) and dark green (FS34079), applied in a wrap-around fashion, though with glossy finish (which certainly contributed to their quite 'tidy' appearance for the duration of their remaining service in Nicaragua). (Artwork by Tom Cooper)

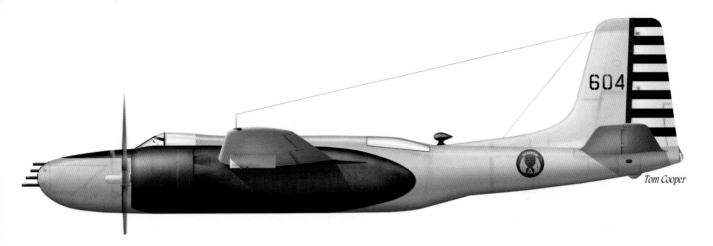

Although the FAN wanted to acquire a sizeable fleet of B-26Bs, it never managed to obtain more than six intact examples, the first four of which were leftovers from Operation *Pluto* – the CIA enterprise that culminated in the Bay of Pigs invasion attempt of Cuba in 1962. Last seen in the mid-1960s, they originally wore serials 400-403. Two B-26Bs obtained from private sources in the USA in 1963 and 1964 were serialed 420 and 423. The four survivors were re-serialed as 601-604 a few years later: the last of these, the B-26B 44-34104, the FAN's 604, was traded to the USA and was still flying in the early 1990s. As far as is known, all wore the same livery of silver-grey overall, with their engine nacelles in matt black. (Artwork by Tom Cooper)

Around the same time it received its first four B-26Bs, the FAN was also donated seven T-28As from the USA. All were painted in silver-grey overall and had wing-tips painted in red, but also had slightly larger black fields on their fuselage sides than usually applied on this type. As became common during the 1960s, the FAN crest – including the actual roundel with the white triangle, surrounded by yellow wings – was worn instead of the national insignia on the fuselage, with national colours down the fin and rudder. The roundels – a blue field outlined in red, with a big white triangle – were applied on the upper left surface of the wing and the bottom of the right wing. Nicaraguan T-28s never received any gun pods, but were frequently armed with launchers for unguided 68mm rockets. (Artwork by Tom Cooper)

The first and only jet 'fighters' operated by the FAN were seven Lockheed T-33Bs acquired in 1963. As usual for this period, all were left in 'bare metal' overall during the first decade of their service, although some examples had parts of their nose painted in red and parts of their wing-tip-mounted drop tanks painted in yellow. Serials – always applied in black on the fin only – were in the range 304-310 (the precise identity of only one aircraft is known: the T-33B with serial 307 was originally the 52-9700 in USAF service). (Artwork by Tom Cooper)

Tom Cooper

In the mid-1970s, the FAN reached a deal with a private contractor in the USA to replace four of its ageing B-26s with eight Cessna 180 Skywagons manufactured in 1959. Operated by the *Escuadrón de Transporte*, they received serials in the range 1000-1007: serial 1005 is known to have been written off on 14 May 1976. The rest of the fleet saw intensive service during the war. As far as is known, all were painted in light grey overall, with an anti-glare panel on the engine cowling. As usual for the time, the national colours on the fin included only three blue stripes. (Artwork by Tom Cooper)

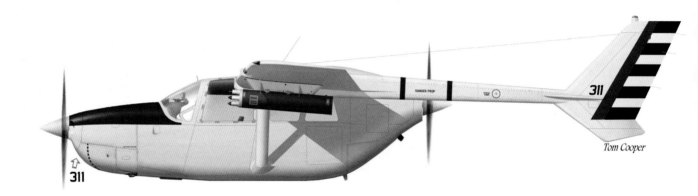

Tom Cooper

The FAN is known to have acquired and operated a total of 10 Cessna 337s from June 1976. While two were written off in 1977 and 1978, the rest of the fleet saw intensive combat service in 1978-79, when at least two, and probably up to four, were shot down by ground fire, while one was flown to Costa Rica by a defecting pilot. All wore the standard livery applied on O-2As operated by the US Air Force, including light grey overall, with dark green anti-glare panel in front of the cockpit. Serials – in the range 311-320 – were applied in black on the front fuselage, below the spinner and on the outer sides of each fin. Usual armament consisted of up to four LAU-3 launchers for unguided 68mm rockets. (Artwork by Tom Cooper)

Tom Cooper

By the mid-1970s, most surviving T-33Bs of the FAN's sole *Escuadrón de Combate* (Combat Squadron) were painted in light blue-grey overall, with a large red strip around the engine exhaust. Other markings remained essentially the same as worn at earlier times. For combat operations, the type was usually armed either with pods for unguided rockets or with US-made bombs such as the Mk.81 (125kg), Mk.82 (250kg) and Mk.83 (500kg). Inset is a detail of the FAN's crest, used instead of the roundel on the rear fuselage. (Artwork by Tom Cooper)

The IAI Arava was a light transport originally designed in Israel. However, the first prototype, designated IAI-101, crashed due to mistakes in construction: the IAI-201 was the result of a complete redesign by Gene Salvay, a highly experienced American aircraft designer working for the Rockwell Corporation detached to Israel to also adapt the US-made J-79 jet engine to the Dassault Mirage fighter – before returning to the USA to design the Rockwell B-1 bomber. Nicaragua placed an order for 14 IAI-201s in 1973, but only one example was delivered. While often reported as wearing either the serial number 223 or 419, all available photographs show it in the livery reconstructed here, with the civilian registration AN-BIR. Note the addition of a pod with Browning M2 machine guns on the fuselage sides, and hardpoints underneath: the latter were frequently used to carry LAU-3 (or similar) pods for unguided 68mm rockets. (Artwork by Tom Cooper)

In 1973, the FAN acquired six de Havilland Canada DHC-3 Otter light transports (also known under the US military designation U-1A). While two were written off under unclear circumstances in 1976, the other four saw intensive service during subsequent years. As far as is known, all were painted either light grey, as shown here, or in light blue-grey overall, and had the bottom sides of their wing-tips painted in day-glo orange, while the top sides might have been painted in white, as shown here. Their serials – always applied in black on the rear fuselage – were in the range 1011-1016. (Artwork by Tom Cooper)

Seven Hughes OH-6As surplus to US Army requirements were donated to Nicaragua in 1975. These entered service with the *Escuadrón de Ala Rotatoria* of the FAN still wearing their original livery of US Army helicopter drab overall, and received serials in the range 511-517. Peacetime and combat attrition (including write-offs of the serial number 511 on 24 March 1971, 516 on 20 August 1975, and 517 on 3 February 1972) soon reduced the fleet, prompting an addition of four H-369HS aircraft (essentially the civilian variant of the OH-6A) in 1977 (serials 528-531). Most known photographs of these helicopters in FAN service showing them wearing not only the usual roundel on the rear fuselage, but also the insignia with the inscription 'ACCIÓN CÍVICA MILITAR' on its upper half and 'AYUDA AL PUEBLO' on the lower half, in white, with the FAN title and roundel. (Artwork by Tom Cooper)

The nascent FAS – the Sandinista Air Force – flew a handful of diverse civilian aircraft, some of which were 'weaponised' for combat purposes. While next to no details about most of them are available, one of the Beech B-55 Barons involved may have looked like this – including a white overall livery, with cheat lines in blue and red – before reportedly receiving a wrap-around camouflage. (Artwork by Tom Cooper)

The heaviest vehicles in GN service were four M4A3 Shermans. Armed with 105mm howitzers, single Shermans saw active combat in 1978 and 1979 on very diverse parts of the Nicaraguan battlefields. All were painted in the same dark green overall, and wore the usual registration numbers, applied in white on forward hull sides. At least three were captured intact by the FSLN. (Artwork by David Bocquelet)

While no precise details about related deliveries are currently available, photographs from several garrisons overrun by the Sandinista in 1979 have shown that the Guardia Nacional received a number of US-made M3 half-tracks. Based on the same photographs, it appears these were painted in green overall. It is probable that at least a few received registration numbers applied in white on the sides of their front armour. (Artwork by David Bocquelet)

In 1957, Nicaragua acquired 68 Chevrolet T17E1 Staghound armoured cars from Israel. About 40 of these were pressed into service, while the rest seem to have been used as sources for spares. Initially, all were painted in olive drab overall. Registration numbers included a prefix PBB followed by the individual vehicle number, and were always applied in white high on the forward hull. Early on, at least the last two figures of the registration number were applied on the centre of the glacis: this registration was later replaced by diverse markings, usually in the form of a triangle, one of which (including the silhouette of a M3 Stuart light tank) is shown in the inset. (Artwork by David Bocquelet)

Sometime in the mid-1970s, surviving Staghounds were all repainted in a darker green overall. They retained their registration numbers: these were applied on all the military vehicles of the GN irrespective of the type, starting sometime in the 1960s, the lowest known being PBB01, worn by a Ford M151 MUTT jeep. Those known to have been applied on the GN's Staghounds ranged from PBB012 up to PBB14x (the final digit of the serial remains unknown). The example with the registration shown here was last seen during operations in the outskirts of Managua in September-October 1978. This artwork shows it as deployed by the insurgency during the battle for León in June 1979, by when it had lost its front fenders but gained the flag of the FSLN for identification purposes. (Artwork by David Bocquelet)

Several photographs showing T17E1 Staghounds captured by the FSLN during the final days of the war (and the insurgent advance into Managua in particular) indicate that at least some of these vehicles received a camouflage pattern consisting of a light sand colour atop their original dark green overall. As usual, all the captured Staghounds were quickly marked as owned by the insurgency – usually in the form of a new 'service title' applied crudely, with brush and white paint, on all four sides of the hull. (Artwork by David Bocquelet)

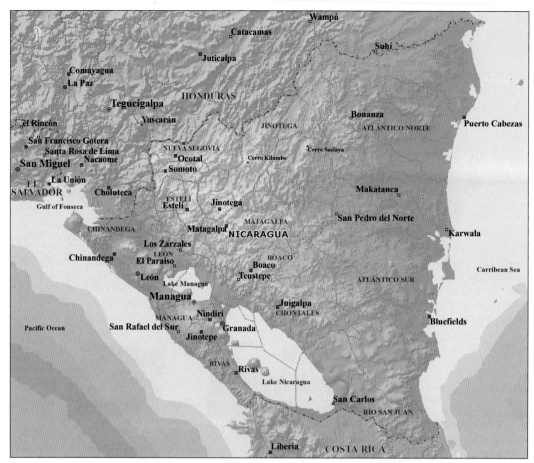

Map of Nicaragua with all major urban centres, departments and major physical features. (Map by Tom Cooper)

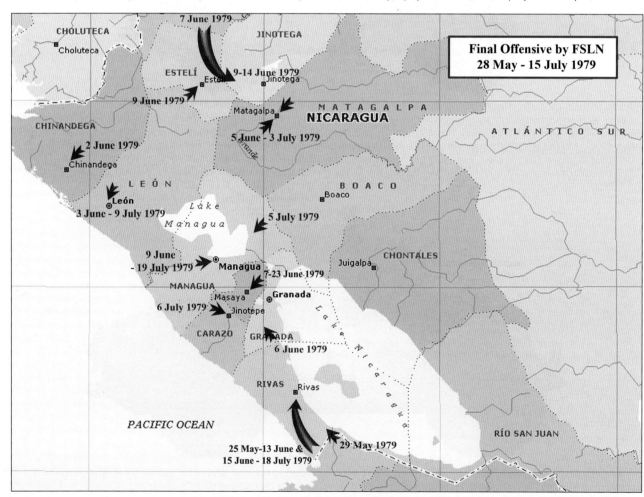

The final offensive of the FSLN, May-July 1979. (Map by Tom Cooper)

José Daniel Ortega Saavedra opposed the Somoza government from an early age and joined the FSLN while a student in 1963. He was arrested and imprisoned from 1967 until 1974. (Mark Lepko Collection)

and later in León. The operation in Estelí, led by the TCU Pedro Altamirano, was the most successful, with a BECAT patrol ambushed and completely annihilated. In Managua, another patrol of BECAT was hit by a grenade near Somoza's home.[180]

In mid-1977 the plan for Operation *October Uprising* was developed in San José, Costa Rica, by Humberto Ortega, Daniel Ortega, Germán Pomares, Victor Tirado, Plutarco Hernandez and Edén Pastora. This envisaged a national insurgency that required taking military barracks, holding positions and fighting the GN on the streets. One of the objectives was to conquer a frontier territory to proclaim a revolutionary government supported by a number of personalities.[181] Although risky, this offensive was well prepared and executed by Tercerists, and ably demonstrated their skill and capability in regards of strategy.[182]

On 12 October 1977, a unit of 40 insurgents – initially led by Daniel Ortega and Víctor Tirado – entered Nicaragua over the northern border near the Las Manos border post, aiming for the town of Ocotal, capital of the Nueva Segovia department. Due to various factors, they failed to adhere to the plan, which included the ambush of a GN patrol in San Fabián, planned for 13 October.[183] Once this attack failed to materialise, Ortega returned to Honduras, while the others split into two rural insurgent units that then ran an 'offensive' on the northern towns for the rest of October and into November.[184] The first of these units, led by Germán Pomares, walked through the Dipilto and Jalapa mountain ranges, launching attacks and harassing GN posts and barracks in Mozonte, Santa Clara and El Limón. On 25 October, three squads led by Pomares seized the city of San Fernando, where GN troops surrendered the local military base. The second column, meanwhile, advanced from Teotecacinte to Macuelizo.

In the south, from Costa Rica, the plan of the uprising was to attack the barracks of San Carlos and Cárdenas, two small border towns, on the same day as the attack in the north. The action was entrusted to the Southern Front, led by the charismatic Edén Pastora Gomez. The attack on the San Carlos barracks was undertaken by Plutarco Hernández, with about 30 fighters recently trained in the use of weapons. They focused on Hacienda La Loma and approached their targets in a vehicle at dawn on 13 October. There were three units: the northernmost unit was charged with the attack on the GN HQ; the central unit, in the east, which was to assault the barracks, was commanded by José Valdivia; and the southern unit, led by Richard Lugo and William Ferrey, were to annihilate the guards outside the HQ. The southern unit eliminated the GN sub-commander, Delgadillo, and the political leader of San Carlos, as well as other guards who

Edén Atanacio Pastora Gomez (also known as 'Commandante Cero'/'Commander Zero' during the insurgency) joined the FSLN while at high school because the Chief of Staff of the GN had murdered his father. (Mark Lepko Collection)

were outside the HQ. The attack on the barracks was also successful. Edén Pastora, meanwhile, attacked Cárdenas.[185]

In the rest of the country, a few days later, raids were launched against GN facilities and other targets, such as a cement factory owned by Somoza. On 15 October, the Masaya barracks, just 20km from the capital, were attacked by Israeli Lewites Rodriguez, at the same time as a major ambush of the GN on the road between Managua and Masaya which killed five soldiers. For four hours, just four guerrillas managed to immobilize all the enemy forces heading from Managua towards Masaya.[186] Barracks were also attacked in Granada. Fighters led by Gaspar García Laviana and Silvio Casco attacked Rivas, while those of Lenin and Jorge Sinforoso targeted Chinandega.

Despite the audacity of these operations, the Sandinistas often failed to seize GN garrisons. In San Carlos, the 50 guerrillas were hunted down after six hours and had to find refuge in Costa Rica. On 17 October, during a clash with the GN on the Masaya-Tipitapa road, Pedro Arauz, a GPP tendency leader, was killed. In Masaya, many Sandinistas cadres were killed or captured during the fighting. In the end, the insurgency was a military failure and a setback for the Tercerists.[187]

The October 1977 offensive nevertheless had the advantage of drawing attention to Nicaragua. On 14 October, a GN plane participating in the bombardment of guerrillas in San Carlos struck three ships on the San Juan and Frío rivers, on which Costa Rican officials were found. San José officially denounced Nicaragua before the OAS for the violation of its territory. Somoza responded by accusing Costa Rica of acting as the FSLN's backbone to attack Nicaragua,[188] also denouncing Cuba for the material and moral support it was giving to the Sandinistas.

The October offensive also allowed the FSLN to arm itself, but the lack of armament remained a major problem for the Sandinistas and prevented them from being able to launch large-scale actions. The Northern Front didn't suffer a single tactical defeat, and the offensive loosened the GN's pressure on the column Pablo Úbeda in the central mountains. In the province of Nueva Segovia, it allowed the guerrillas to move closer to the economic, social and political centres and to exercise greater influence. While the offensive relied heavily on traditional guerrilla warfare, it also allowed the FSLN to move to areas of greater political influence. The FSLN launched this offensive with only 150 fighters, but managed to recruit 300-400 new fighters while suffering minimal combat losses.[189] Theirs forces had not been broken and they had acquired weapons. They also gave evidence of their firepower and their ability to manoeuvre, hit, retreat, build strength and strike again without loss. They showed above all the FSLN's ability to attack throughout the country, and with the establishment of the Northern Front to organize a permanent guerrilla zone in the north of the country, even though the offensive was only a clash between the guerrillas and the GN while the population at large remained spectators for the most part.[190].

The October offensive was also a Tercerist manoeuvre to force other FSLN tendencies to adopt the strategy they proposed. They were convinced that the regime's crisis was so profound that the opportunity to overthrow it could not be missed. For this they had to push other tendencies to abandon their defensive positions. Some sectors of the Nicaraguan left, including the communists and even some FSLN members, criticized the October offensive, describing it as 'adventurous' and detrimental to the development of the mass movement.[191] Nevertheless, for the Tercerists it had the merit of avoiding a 'bourgeois democratic exit' to the crisis of the regime at a moment when the civil opposition received Washington's support.

The Carter administration policy and Somoza's departure to the US following a heart attack undermined the dictatorship. For the bourgeois opposition, this was an opportunity to take the initiative. Under the authority of Archbishop Obando y Bravo, it formed a committee for national dialogue which aimed to promote political reforms in a peaceful way. Bringing together clergymen, teachers, businessmen and industrialists, the committee wanted to end corruption, ensure respect for human rights and guarantee that 1980 presidential elections would be run honestly. The committee received support from the UDEL and met the US ambassador to Managua to push Washington to play a more active role.[192]

The FSLN took advantage of this climate to get closer to the moderate civilian opposition. For this, they relied on left-wing intellectuals, progressive priests, conservatives and a businessman who formed a group called *Los Doce* (The Twelve), who affirmed in a manifesto of 14 October their support for the FSLN's goals.[193] Somoza ordered their arrest and in late 1977 they fled to Costa Rica, from where they wrote a proclamation of support for the Sandinistas, specifying that the FSLN had participate in the solution of Nicaragua's problems. The Sandinistas thus came out of their political isolation and quickly took a central place in the political game.

Chamorro's Murder

At the end of 1977, the pressure upon Somoza was greater than ever before. Nevertheless, when approached by the Archbishop Obando committee, he rejected the proposal to open negotiations with the opposition. The Carter administration – which saw an opportunity to get rid of Somoza – maintained pressure through the US ambassador to Managua. Finally, in December, the dictator accepted that discussions would begin after the municipal elections in February 1978. However, the situation was completely upset on 10 January 1978 when Chamorro, the UDEL leader, was murdered on a Managua street by three unknown men.[194] National and international public opinion accused Somoza of his murder. For Nicaraguans, the dictator had committed sacrilege, which resulted in a prompt rapprochement

Pedro Joaquín Chamorro Cardenal was a journalist and editor of *La Prensa*, the only significant opposition newspaper during the decades of the Somoza rule. (Courtesy *El 19*)

between his opponents.[195] Indeed, the UDEL quickly decided to withdraw from negotiations initiated by the Obando committee.

The death of Chamorro provoked riots in Managua, while union and employee leaders launched a general strike on 24 January. The strike was massive: it affected up to 50% of companies and business in Managua and over 80% elsewhere around the country. In the industrial zone of Managua, people threw Molotov cocktails at factories belonging to the dictator. Somoza responded to the agitation with fierce repression. The GN fired on the rioters, and took action to prevent a strike by 12,000 workers in the oil refinery in Managua. The media underwent censorship to avoid disseminating information on the strike.[196]

The FSLN that came out of its October offensive relied on this agitation to stir up the rejection of the dictatorship. Its fighting units were strategically located in the country. There was the Northern Front, the Pablo Úbeda Front to the north-east, the Rigoberto López Perez Front in the west and the Zeledon Benjamín Front in the south. The north of the country was the safest zone for the FSLN, where Amerindians, peasants and agricultural workers of the haciendas supported the Sandinistas and were recruited into the ranks of the guerrillas. These new forces enabled the Sandinistas to launch new actions at the end of January 1978.[197]

The FSLN demonstrated its military capabilities by launching raids in different parts of the country. In the north-west, the Sandinistas attacked a bank and a GN convoy near Chinandega. In León, fights against the GN lasted for two days, with 14 fighters killed and 24 wounded. In the south-west, on 2 February, about 30 guerrillas led by Camilo Ortega seized the GN garrison in Granada before being driven out after two hours. In the north, the FSLN attacked the Santa Clara anti-guerrilla camp in the Nueva Segovia department, an action led by Germán Pomares, Victor Tirado and Daniel Ortega.[198]

On 3 February, a group of about 30 guerrillas from Costa Rica under the leadership of Edén Pastora and the priest Gaspar García Laviana attacked the border town of Peñas Blancas and joined FSLN units present in the region. Between 60 and 100 fighters then launched an attack against the Rivas garrison south of Granada, being finally repulsed by the Somoza forces after four hours of fighting. In the north of the country, FSLN commandos attacked military posts all along the border with Honduras.

The death of Chamorro caused an insurrection in Masaya, starting with a general strike that affected up to 95% of local trade: not only workers in most local businesses, but even doctors and nurses issued separate statements of support for the strike, mass demonstrations took place every day and became radicalized with the construction of barricades. The GN reacted with brutal repression, killing at least two – including Santiago Potosme – while injuring dozens and detaining hundreds. However, there was no let up: Postome's funeral on 6 February was converted into another mass demonstration. Somoza ordered more vicious action, and the next morning the population of Masaya woke up to find their town besieged by the military. It took several days for the opposition to reorganize, but by 15 February the residents began throwing Molotov cocktails at homes of regime supporters and their relatives. In turn, the GN assaulted and scattered a religious service for Chamorro five days later, wounding more than 200 in the process.

Just when it appeared that the general strike might run out of steam, there was a new escalation in Monimbó,

A typical example of stone barricades, widely constructed during the popular uprising in Monibó, in the Masaya department, in February 1978. (via Mark Lepko)

a district of Masaya containing about 20,000 indigenous people. On 21 February, a commemoration of the anniversary of Sandino's assassination was organized, prompting the GN to attack and scatter the crowd, which provoked fire-fights with the Indians lasting several days. The insurgents meanwhile began organizing themselves by the blocks and quarters in which they lived: they eventually established themselves in control of all the key points of Monimbó, encircling the entire neighbourhood with stone barricades.[199] Inside the 'liberated zone' created in this fashion, all the detained henchmen of the regime were executed.

As the GN proved unable to re-establish control and patrol more than downtown Masaya, the uprising – which was entirely spontaneous, without any links to the FSLN – continued to spread. The revolt extended to the Indians of Sbtiava near León and those of Diriamba and Jinotepe in the province of Carazo. Armed clashes in these towns were sporadic by nature, but Monimbó remained the hotbed of resistance. The FSLN sent Camilo Ortega to the town in an attempt to direct the insurrection. At this point, on 26 February, the GN reacted with an all-out assault, supported by armour and air strikes, violently crushing the uprising and killing more than 80.[200] Even Camilo Ortega found himself cornered in the town of Catarina, and was eventually killed. The FSLN avenged his death by assassinating General Reynaldo Pérez Vega, Chief of Staff of the GN, 10 days later.

While the government thus managed to recover control of Masaya, demonstrations continued. In April, the situation in Estelí reached boiling point after the GN violently crushed a demonstration by the local children. The protesters reacted with attacks on the houses of the Somozists, looting and riots, which continued into early May.[201]

The insurgency of Monimbó reinforced the Tercerist strategy of running an insurrection in urban areas. Indeed, they subsequently dissolved their units in northern Nicaragua and redeployed their combatants to Estelí, León and Managua to form resistance cells for a future urban insurrection.[202] Their emphasis on urban insurgency rather than guerrilla warfare in the countryside was causing greater loss of life because it made repression easier, especially with aerial bombardment of urban neighbourhoods. However, the net result was that from May 1978, the construction of barricades and street fights in working-class neighbourhoods all around Nicaragua greatly

increased.

Overall, between March and July 1978, the FSLN managed to increase its influence. Mass protests, demonstrations and armed clashes against government forces resulted in ever larger numbers of activists rallying to the armed opposition. Above all, they allowed the Sandinistas to take control of the insurrectional climate that was taking hold and to find new leaders for the movement. Henceforth, they were able to campaign in neighbourhoods, high schools and universities, but also to recruit workers of many companies and organize the population of dozens of neighbourhoods into Civil Defence Committees.[203] In high schools, young people were organized in the MES for the Proletarian Tendency, or the Association of Secondary Students for the GPP Tendency. Universities had the Revolutionary Student Front for the GPP Tendency and the FER-ML for the Proletarians. In the unions, in addition to the traditional organizations linked to the PSN, the FSLN was present in the Workers Union Movement (GPP) and the committees of the revolutionary workers (Proletarians).

In this climate, disagreements between the FSLN factions tended to gradually fade as the political situation hardened. The GPP Tendency continued its efforts in rural areas while increasing its actions among urban populations. It also gave up its vision of a possible insurgency only in the long term to consider this one in a shorter time. The Proletarian Tendency, while continuing to favour the urban proletariat, gave greater attention to rural workers. The Tercerists were reinforced with new militants impatient for a revolution that seemed closer than ever. Finally, the different FSLN tendencies became closer, and at a secret conference in Costa Rica in July, the representatives of the three tendencies signed an agreement that provided for the formation of a general coordination committee to organize tactical cooperation, each tendency retaining the freedom to determine its tactics employed in military operations.

During the spring and summer of 1978, most FSLN military activity was carried out by the columns of the Northern and Nueva-Guinea Fronts in rural and mountainous areas. The combat actions were quite limited because of the ability of the GN to maintain control over strategic areas, which forced the guerrillas to keep a defensive position. Fighting was therefore concentrated north of the El Espino border crossing in the province of Madriz and around Estelí. To the south, the FSLN launched attacks from Costa Rica on El Castillo in the province of Rio San Juan. The most spectacular action during this period took place in Managua, when two Sandinistas fired two rockets from the Intercontinental Hotel on the Somoza headquarters known as the Bunker. One of the rockets didn't explode, while the other struck a GN building without causing any casualties.[204]

In July, under pressure from the Carter administration, Somoza accepted the return to Nicaragua of members of the *Los Doce* group, who had sought refuge in Costa Rica. On 16 July, they held a rally in Estelí before going to Monimbó, the centre of Indian resistance in Somoza. On the political front, *Los Doce* joined the Broad Opposition Front (*Frente Amplio Opositor*, FAO) formed earlier in the year, which brought together the centrist and leftist opposition in Somoza. The FAO included the UDEL, the Nicaraguan Democratic Movement moderate organizations, trade unions and student groups. Above all, it received the support of the Tercerists, with whom links were forged.[205]

4

THE SEPTEMBER 1978 OFFENSIVE

The year 1978 marked an acceleration of the Nicaraguan crisis. Washington began to imagine how to remove Somoza and saw the bourgeois opposition as an alternative. The Sandinistas did not initiate events at the beginning of the year, only reacting to diverse developments. There was great danger that they would be ousted from their predominant place in the fight against Somoza. Thus, they were forced to take the initiative – and did so, late in the summer of the same year.

Operation Chanchera

On 22 August 1978, Edén Pastora, 'Commander Zero', led a group of 24 guerrillas of the Rigoberto Lopez Perez commando in an action against the National Palace, seat of the Congress of Nicaragua. Pastora was assisted by Hugo Torres ('Commander Uno') and Dora María Tellez Argüello ('Commander Dos'). The action had been prepared since May, when Pastora arrived from Costa Rica. Between 5-12 August, the 25 members of the commando, divided into two teams, found shelter to complete their training and preparation for their mission. On 22 August they went to the National Palace in two fake Army vehicles and dressed in GN uniforms. At 1230 hours, the two groups of guerrillas entered the Palace through the east and west side doors. Pastora killed a GN who tried to intervene and the whole commando reached the Congress on the second floor, where they took 40 congressmen prisoner, as well as the Ministers of the Interior and Finance. In only a few minutes the National Palace had passed into Sandinista control.

Approximately 280 GN soldiers commanded by Michael Echannis, supported by armoured vehicles and planes, then surrounded the building.[206] A GN helicopter strafed the palace, injuring several civilians and killing at least two people. Somoza decreed a state of siege and sent GN troops into other major cities of the country as a precaution. In the National Palace, the insurgent commandos took between 1,500 and 2,000 people as hostage.

Negotiations began, with the Archbishop of Managua and the Bishops of León and Granada designated as mediators between the Sandinistas and the government. The former demanded an amnesty for political prisoners, the release of 100 Sandinista prisoners, the dissemination of FSLN communiqués by the media, the establishment of a neutral zone between those held by the GN and those of the guerrillas, a ransom of US$10 million and a safe conduct for the commando that held the National Palace.[207]

Somoza obtained the release of 100 employees of the Palace, women and children. The Sandinistas also released about 15 wounded and the bodies of the eight GN troops killed during the attack. About 25 hostages managed to escape from the building through an open window. In order to put pressure on Somoza, Pastora threatened to execute two Liberal Party congressmen and a journalist from the pro-government newspaper *Novedades*. An agreement was finally

A GN truck carrying troops for one of many interventions in response to the outbreak of violence in August 1978. (Albert Grandolini Collection)

A column of Dodge WC-series 4WD trucks with GN troops racing towards the National Palace in Managua on 22 August 1978. (via Mark Lepko)

reached on 23 August, with the required ransom decreased from $10 million to $500,000. On the 24th, members of the commando, accompanied by 59 released Sandinista prisoners - including Tomás

A CH-34/S-55 helicopter of the FAN evacuating bodies of GN troops killed during the assault on the National Palace. (Pit Weinert Collection)

Somoza with an S-55T during negotiations in front of the National Palace (for a reconstruction of this Choctaw, see the colour section of the book). (Pit Weinert Collection)

Borge - the ecclesiastical negotiators, the ambassador of Panama and a Venezuelan diplomat embarked on two Venezuelan Hercules planes heading for Panama. Upon arrival, 22 of the released prisoners fled to Cuba.[208]

The takeover of the Palace transformed the state of mind of the population and aroused international interest in the FSLN struggle. It increased the myth of FSLN invincibility among the masses, demonstrating great pragmatism, political sense and military tenacity that surrounded the Sandinistas with a kind of heroic aura. It also gave a new militant impulse that strengthened all forms and fronts of the struggle. The FAO called for a general strike on 27 August, the announcement of which was enough to provoke trouble in Matagalpa, where young boys armed themselves and built barricades.[209] The students ambushed BECAT squads with bombs, and there were incidents of firing against the GN. The population built barricades and violent fights ensued. The GN garrison was besieged, forcing Somoza to send reinforcements and launch air attacks against insurgent positions, killing about 50 and wounding some 200 in five days. Similar events affected the cities of Diriamba, Estelí, Jinotepe and León. In Managua, GN installations were attacked by around 5,000 young people supported by 400 Sandinistas guerrillas. The capture of the National Palace had put an end to the FSLN's defensive posture.[210]

Alarmed by the worsening situation in Nicaragua and supported by the Carter administration, Venezuela called for the UN Security Council and OAS to take steps to resolve the Nicaraguan crisis. For its part, Costa Rica, which feared the unrest that affected its neighbour would overflow the border, asked the OAS to initiate a peace plan. In mid-September the OAS decided to send an inspection mission to investigate incidents around the border between Costa Rica and Nicaragua.

September offensive

Eager to keep the political and military initiative after taking the National Palace and the Matagalpa uprising, the FSLN launched a new popular uprising in several cities on 9 September 1978, for which the Sandinistas decided to concentrate their forces. Those from Granada were sent to Masaya, while those from the north of the country were concentrated in Estelí. The goal was to launch an insurgency in Masaya, Managua, León, Chinandega and Estelí. In the south, troops were gathered to hit Penas-Blancas and then advance on Rivas.[211]

In Managua there were attacks against five police stations, while urban combat units composed of 30 men led by Joaquin Cuadra Lacayo and Óscar Pereira Perezcassar faced the GN in the neighbourhoods of Las Americas, San Judas and Open 3. The objective was to retain GN troops in the capital as other cities rose up. Of the five police stations attacked, only two were taken with their weapons confiscated.[212]

In Masaya, where the Sandinistas had the Rufo Marin combat unit, which included up to 15 armed men, the insurrection led by Hilarío Sánchez Vásquez and Ulises Tapia Roa[213] began with the taking of the GN HQ in Monimbó. On 10 September, the insurgents attacked the central barracks. The regime could not tolerate such acts of rebellion only 30km from Managua.

In León, the FSLN squads, led by Roger Dishón Argüello and Carlos Manuel Jarquín, attacked the GN barracks and the prison and took control of certain neighbourhoods. In Chinandega, the Proletarian Tendency dominated. They had many networks, activists and fighters in this city grouped in the *Comandos Revolucionaríos del Pueblo*, that also existed in the nearby port city of Corinto. The guerrillas, under the command of Blas Real Espinales, took control of the city and held it for four days, facing EEBI troops supported by helicopters before retreating to Honduras.

In Estelí, Northern Front forces composed of 27 guerrillas from the column Jorge Sinforoso Bravo, under the command of Francisco Rivera ('El Zorro'), launched an insurgency on 9 September. The city, bordered by the highway that leads to the northern border, was a strategic location. The column was divided into four guerrilla groups: the first was on the northern route, led by Facundo Picado, to contain the GN from Ocotal, Madriz and Condega; the second was in south, towards Santa Cruz, facing the GN from Matagalpa and Managua; the third group, under the command of Rivera, attacked the GN HQ in Estelí; while the fourth remained in reserve.[214] They were joined by the squadron Pedro Altamirano, commanded by Julio César Ramos, for an attack against the headquarters of the GN on 10 September.[215]

Although the dictatorship was initially destabilized by these events, it quickly regained the initiative. With the insurrectional experiences of October 1977 and February 1978, Somoza decided to act strongly. He first decreed a state of emergency in the provinces of Masaya and Estelí before extending it to the whole country. He also mobilized 3,000 GN Reservists.[216] His strategy was simple: gather his forces to take the insurgent cities one after the other. After quickly taking control of Managua, he launched his troops, including armoured Shermans, against Masaya, which he considered strategically important. The city underwent aerial bombardments[217] like those in Chinandega. The EEBI moved forward, and after three days of combat FSLN fighters had to retreat. The district of Monimbó was in ruins but the regime had achieved its goal. Subsequently, Somoza wanted to make Masaya one of his strongholds, installing General Fermín Meneses and a supply centre for troops in the south of the country.[218]

Three days after taking over Masaya, Somoza's soldiers attacked

A still from a video showing troops of the GN raiding the outskirts of Managua in September 1978. (via Mark Lepko)

A close-up view of one of two Staghounds during the same action, showing its registration: PB8099. (via Mark Lepko)

Another still from the same video, showing the rest of the column – including GN troops wearing flak vests and at least two Staghound armoured cars. (via Mark Lepko)

A FAN C-47 passing low over the burning outskirts of Managua during the September 1978 offensive. (Pit Weinert Collection)

León and then Estelí, from where, following air strikes, the guerrillas retreated to rural areas, also retreating from all urban areas in the Jinotega department. There were many civilian casualties when the EEBI attacked on 17 September with tanks and guns, killing 180 civilians and injuring a further 200 in northern Estelí.

On 19 September the GN regained control of all the towns attacked by the FSLN, but intense fighting continued. In Estelí, many people followed the guerrillas when they evacuated the city and joined their cause. In a camp set up by the FSLN south of Estelí, there were nearly 180 people, many of them women. This exodus strengthened the Northern Front with hundreds of new fighters who had to be trained for combat.[219]

In the south of the country, on 13 September, the forces of the Southern Front guerrillas - about 200 men commanded by Daniel Ortega, Victor Tirado and Edén Pastora - left Costa Rica and attacked GN barracks in Sapoa and Peñas Blancas in the Rivas department.[220] The GN concentrated its forces in Cibalsa and the port of San Juan del Sur. After a day of combat in which the GN held their positions successfully, the guerrillas were forced to flee to their Costa Rican sanctuary. However, the Costa Rican authorities apprehended them and expelled them to Panama.

The September offensive marked a worsening in the already poor relationship between Nicaragua and Costa Rica, where Sandinistas guerrillas set up assembly areas before crossing the border to launch attacks. The FAN launched raids into Costa Rica on 12 and 13 September. Costa Rica felt particularly vulnerable because it was defended by only 5,000 men of its civil guard. To ensure its safety, on 15 September it signed a mutual defence agreement with Venezuela, which sent four fighter planes, while Panama lent several combat helicopters. Meanwhile, the OAS condemned Nicaragua for its air raids in Costa Rica.

The insurrection of September 1978 strengthened the Sandinistas. The convergence of the various tendencies that had emerged at this time was the first step in overcoming the split in the FSLN. On the military side, it allowed the group to improve the quality and quantity of its forces. It now had more fighters, more weapons, more combat experience and more spirit of victory. Tercerists also managed to organize a radio communication system with each Front,[221] while all tendencies had undergone general fighting training and increased offensive actions of all types and sizes.

The September offensive was above all a demonstration that the urban masses were able to rebel. But it also showed that it was a mistake to launch attacks all over the country at the same time, as Somoza's forces had the opportunity to regroup and attack the Sandinistas one after the other, maintaining their mobility and the initiative. This lesson was learned by the FSLN for its offensive in 1979. The price to pay was nevertheless heavy, since according to the Red Cross 5,000 civilians were killed, 10,000 wounded and 25,000 made homeless.[222]

The September offensive also had the effect of forcing Washington to intervene. A few days after the beginning of the Sandinista offensive, the US tried to establish a mediation to solve the crisis in Nicaragua. On 17 September, William Jorden, US ambassador to Panama, began a tour of Colombia, Venezuela, Panama, Costa Rica, El Salvador, Honduras and Mexico to obtain support for a negotiated settlement of the crisis. On 25 September, he finally met Somoza, who a week later accepted mediation.[223] The mission included US Ambassador William Bowdler, Foreign Minister Ramón Emilio Jiménez of the Dominican Republic and Alfredo Obiols Gómez, former Minister of Foreign Affairs of Guatemala. For the opposition, the chosen mediators were Alfonso Robelo Callejas from the MDN, Sergio Ramírez Mercado from *Los Doce* and Rafael Cordova Rivas from the UDEL. The FSLN opposed the mediation as a manoeuvre aimed at preventing them from achieving their objectives of military victory and the overthrow of Somoza. Despite this opposition, the Tercerists continued to maintain contacts with the mediators, including Sergio Ramírez.[224]

The arrival of international mediators in Managua on 6 October provoked suspicion and disunity within the Nicaraguan opposition. Unanimity existed only on one point, the necessity of the resignation of Somoza. The FAO requested a transition to the presidential election in September 1981, with the resignation and departure of Somoza. In case of refusal, the Congress would vote for the impeachment of Somoza. A member of Congress would be chosen as interim president by a Council of State consisting of two members of the FAO and the Liberal Party. Somoza immediately rejected this proposal.[225]

The US proposed the organization of a plebiscite where the whole population would decide the future of Somoza and the nation. In response, on 10 November the dictator proposed a plebiscite to choose members of the opposition who would share power with him. The FAO rejected this counter-proposal that would allow Somoza to stay in power. The FAO also announced that it would leave the mediation if Somoza didn't resign before 21 November. International mediators asked the dictator to reconsider his decision not to resign, while the Carter administration also pressured Somoza. Economic and military assistance were suspended, while the International Monetary Fund postponed the granting of a $20 million loan to Managua. On 12 November, negotiations were suspended to allow Bowdler to travel to Washington for consultations with the Secretary of State. On 18 November, the OAS Human Rights Commission published a report denouncing the abuses and violations of the Somoza regime and recommended sanctions.[226]

Back in Nicaragua, Bowdler failed to reach a compromise for the organization of a plebiscite, while the FAO withdrew from negotiations on 21 November. Nevertheless, international mediators unveiled a peace plan on 22 November called the Washington Plan. It proposed the organization within 60 days, under international control, of a plebiscite to decide Nicaragua's future. To ensure free elections, Somoza had to suspend martial law, allow the exercise of constitutional freedoms, announce an amnesty for political prisoners, allow the return of exiles, allow international control over the media and confine the GN to its barracks. Somoza refused the Washington Plan on 24 November, but the mediators gave him an ultimatum to accept it within 72 hours, threatening to withdraw if he did not. Somoza finally accepted the principle of a plebiscite. Between 1 December 1978 and 19 January 1979, when the mediators acknowledged their failure, Somoza rejected the conditions imposed by the opposition to ensure a free and open ballot. The dictator even refused to agree that the electoral process be supervised by OAS. Faced with the failure of all attempts at mediation, Washington raised the tone against Somoza. On 8 February 1979, half of the US government employees in Nicaragua were recalled to the United States, while military assistance was cancelled and economic assistance frozen.[227]

The failure of mediation strengthened the FSLN's desire to impose itself on the military. Internally, the Tercerist strategy gradually imposed itself on all tendencies. The proletarian faction announced the beginning of a war of attrition against the regime, avoiding direct confrontations in favour of harassment tactics. Since the

September 1978 uprising, the GPP Tendency had been reconsidering its mountain-based strategy, despite opposition from such as Omar Cabezas, who was on Kilambé Hill. The leaders of the column General Pedro Altamirano pressed the National Directorate and the other columns to redirect their actions towards the cities.[228]

This rallying to Tercerist positions was not without self-interest. The Sandinistas were beginning to receive external support in terms of equipment, weapons and also fighters, such as the Victoriano Brigade, which arrived in Nicaragua on 27 September to join the Central Front. Other Tendencies also wanted to benefit from this supply.

Towards a permanent insurrection

The FSLN wanted to continue to keep pressure on Somoza to prevent him from taking the initiative and especially to avoid a political solution under the auspices of Washington which would have excluded its involvement in power-sharing. It therefore designated the highly successful Edén Pastora as commander-in-chief of Sandinista forces. Under his command were the Northern Front, Western Front and Central Front – a total of about 2,000 combatants. In turn, Somoza developed a plan to double the GN to about 15,000 troops.[229]

Sandinista armed actions continued to intensify. On 15 October 1978, the FSLN attacked GN troops in Monimbó and Santa María near Masaya, destroying three trucks. Three days later, four guerrillas attacked an American bank in Managua, stealing US$100,000, while on 27 October they robbed an armoured van carrying US$150,000 in cheques and securities. On 23 November, the Southern Front launched an attack against the Pueblo Nuevo GN headquarters in the Guadalupe Valley. In the north, on 26 November, after crossing the Honduran border, guerrillas attacked the GN base in Achuapa before returning to Honduras. A week later, they launched a new raid against Achuapa. The GN decided to use aviation to fight the Sandinistas in the region. On 12 December, air attacks were launched against FSLN bases in the Guaylo Valley, about 300km north of Managua.[230]

Three days later, in the south, the Sandinistas attacked the GN post in La Pimenta near the Costa Rican border. From 16 to 17 December 1978, a battle occurred near the Río El Naranjo. The Southern Front organized groups by zones, with group 1 near Peñas Blancas, group 10 between Peñas Blancas and the Pacific, group 12 further east and group 13 near Colon. From its positions, the FSLN bombed Peñas Blancas for a week with 70mm mortars. These attacks forced the closure of the Peñas Blancas border for a week on 22 December 1978.[231]

Elsewhere in the country, some 30 guerrillas took control of an Indian community just 25km from Managua on 26 December, killing two GN informants. At the same time, another Sandinista commando seized a radio station in Matagalpa, from where it broadcast their

The reaction by Somoza and the GN to the insurgent offensive of September 1978 was vicious, characterised by mass atrocities against the Nicaraguan population. Here mothers ask troops about the fate of their missing children. (courtesy of Instituto de Historia Militar)

According to official releases from Managua, between September and December 1978 the GN "stamped out rebellion with overwhelming firepower and air support". The operation in question was characterised by a massive deployment of the military, supported by heavy weapons – including M4A3 Shermans – on the streets, and an unprecedented campaign of terror and mass murder. (Mark Lepko Collection)

One of the FAN's O-2As involved in air strikes on the Guaylo Valley in northern Nicaragua in December 1978. (via Mark Lepko)

propaganda. Guerrillas confronted the GN in the city of León on 18 December, while on 31 December they attacked the GN after it discovered a guerrilla training camp in Estelí. At the end of 1978, Somoza nevertheless remained confident in the GN's ability to defeat the FSLN in 1979.

The dictator felt strong enough to threaten to invade Costa Rica, which broke diplomatic relations with Managua, closed the border at Peñas Blancas and asked the OAS to deploy observers.[232] The first of these – all civilians – arrived on 30 December. Nevertheless, the Sandinistas continued to harass the GN's post in Río Sabalo from Costa Rica. On 13 January, the squad Ramón Raudales harassed the Cardenas HQ and managed to damage a 'push and pull' jet. On 14 January, there was another attack on Peñas Blancas. Similarly, in the north, during the first 10 days of January 1979, the FSLN launched attacks on a dozen villages in the north of the Estelí and León departments. The GN responded with rockets and machine guns, killing many civilians. In Managua, the guerrillas dynamited a radio station belonging to the Somoza family. They confronted the GN in Chinandega and León, destroying government properties and organizing propaganda meetings.

Sandinista pressure was becoming stronger, and in León the different combat units were ordered to maintain the offensive. Militia units were in permanent struggles, and the GN could no longer enter certain neighbourhoods. These units carried out two major ambushes during this period. The first took place on 28 April in La Barranca, with several combat units, and the second on 18 May in San Pedro, with the use of RPG-2 and Claymore mines. They also attacked the Posultega HQ with two or three combat units. The FSLN in León had six combat units properly organized with their commanders, all their structures and well-trained fighters.[233]

As 21 February approached, the 45th anniversary of Sandino's death, the FSLN's actions were growing in frequency and scale across the country. The actions of the guerrillas included daily attacks on GN troops and installations, attacks on banks, the confiscation of medical supplies in hospitals, the takeover of radio stations for propaganda broadcasts, the sabotage of enterprises and agricultural properties and the assassination of Somoza's supporters. Fighting between the FSLN and GN was particularly fierce in Matagalpa, León, Granada, Masaya, Diriamba, Chichigalpa, Estelí, Chinandega, Managua and along the Costa Rica border throughout February and into March. More than 100 guerrillas attacked and seized the cities of El Sauce in the province of León and El Jícaro in Nueva Segovia, managing to keep control of it for 10 days.[234] Popular militias were mobilized for small harassment operations. The GN thus found itself dispersed to face these actions, mobilized permanently without being able to take rest, with a demoralizing effect on the soldiers.[235]

The main objective of these many actions was to maintain the insurgency climate which had taken hold of Nicaragua since the beginning of 1978. The FSLN also wanted to train its fighters before the final offensive and, taking lessons from those of 1977 and 1978, it put into practice the tactics of dispersion of the GN by the multiplication of attacks around the whole country.

The Sandinista strategy in spring 1979

With the failure of Washington's mediation attempt at the end of 1978, Somoza decided to stay in power at all costs and tried to provoke US military intervention. Meanwhile, the US reinforced its support for the bourgeois opposition forces but also for the GN to avoid its disappearance, that would have plunged the country into chaos. Somoza could count on the GN's loyalty, the support of the Nationalist Liberal Party, officials and some of the conservatives. Facing him was the legal opposition, based on the forces of the reformist bourgeoisie opposition gathered in the FAO. This moderate opposition also included the Catholic Church, headed by Archbishop Obando y Bravo. On the national scene, the Somoza regime also had to tolerate a legal Sandinista bloc with the emergence of a new opposition group, called the MPU (*Movimiento Pueblo Unido*, United People's Movement), founded on 14 June 1978. Led by the son of Chamorro, it brought together student organizations, trade unions and large numbers of the urban poor.[236] The MPU became the backbone of a larger opposition gathering known as the *Frente Patriotico Nacional* (FPN, National Patriotic Front). The birth of the FPN was the symptom of a radicalization of the civil opposition. It received the support of the *Los Doce* group, Sandinista student and worker organizations such as the Committees of Revolutionary Workers and the trade union movement, but also organizations close to the FSLN such as the PSN, the Association of Women Confronting the National Problem (AMPRONAC) and progressive teacher organizations.[237] The FPN was one of the most powerful opposition organizations, an opposition markedly to the left and favourable to the Sandinistas.

Meanwhile, the FSLN's reunification process continued. It was realized partly under pressure from Fidel Castro, who conditioned the continuation of military support to the reunification of the Sandinistas.[238] The three tendencies signed a unity pact on 8 March, providing for the creation of a joint National Directorate, with three members from each tendency to oversee and coordinate the organization's activities. Each tendency nevertheless continued to exist in distinct ways. This reunification was the price to be paid by the Tercerists for endorsement of their plan of general insurrection.[239] On the military side, a national joint staff was set up in Managua and then in each zone of the country, allowing the unification of all the Sandinista armed forces.[240]

In January 1979, a meeting of Tercerist leaders was held in Panama, where plans for a general insurrection were designed. The Sandinista strategy aimed to disperse the GN forces throughout the country while structuring and consolidating the guerrilla fronts.[241] The FSLN wanted to carry out blows relentlessly, maintaining an offensive posture to accelerate the wear and tear of the enemy by using insurgencies in cities and urban and rural guerrillas. Until then the Sandinista forces were fighting in the cities within the limits of how well they could 'disappear' into the local population, with small mobile groups to strike the enemy. Tercerists aimed their operations on a larger scale requiring the mobilization of more numerous, better-armed units. They wanted, within 30-45 days, to complete a strategic encirclement of Managua, to defeat the enemy or force their surrender. For this, the Sandinista contingent was about 5,000 organized fighters in early 1979, of which about 2,000 were armed with guns, the rest with light weapons.

The general plan of insurrection attributed to each front a particular mission. The Northern Front, by its geographical position, manoeuvrability and firepower, had to play the main role. Its task was to attract the enemy forces as much as possible. The Southern Front was to fix in the isthmus of Rivas the best GN troops, while the Central Front's main mission was to organize the revolt of the popular districts of the capital and thus fix a part of the enemy forces there. The Eastern Front, which included the territories of Masaya, Carazo and Granada, was to hinder ground communications between Managua and Rivas, as well as the dictatorship's aerial logistics, and eventually seize the town of Masaya. The Western Front's strategic mission was to stage uprisings in León and Chinandega. The South-Eastern Front Roberto Huembes was formed in the Chontales region, while the small guerrillas were reactivated in the Minas-Atlantic region.[242]

The FSLN leadership installed its command post in Palo Alto, Costa Rica. This base was organized as a small complex, with three factories and warehouses scattered in different parts of Costa Rica. In one of them, the FSLN had a wireless communication system connected with all the Fronts. In 1979 the Sandino Radio, operated from the hacienda '*La Lucha*' which belonged to José Figueres, encouraged the fighters with its propaganda, especially through songs of Carlos and Luis Enrique Mejia Godoy and others.

To weaken the Somoza regime, the FSLN's national leadership decided to attack the country's economy in mid-March by striking a key export sector, cotton.[243] The Western Front reported that on 7 March the combat unit Julio Cesar Chavez attacked the San José Ginning Plant in La Paz Centro, destroying machinery and a large amount of stored cotton. The guerrillas destroyed a further 6,000 bales of cotton and damaged multiple farms and industrial facilities while attacking producers in the provinces of León and Chinandega. This was a hard blow for the economy, since cotton exports represent a third of Nicaragua's foreign trade. Managua had no longer been able to cope with the repayment of its debt in November 1978, while Washington froze a loan of US$10 million following the failure of the attempted mediation.[244] While experiencing the effects of the country's economic deterioration, Somoza was forced at the same time to continue conducting a costly military effort against a rapidly spreading insurgency, which was now openly operating in urban centres across the country.

5

FROM THE SPRING OFFENSIVE TO THE GENERAL UPRISING

At the beginning of 1979, all the conditions seemed to be in place to defeat Somoza, who found himself totally isolated. Nevertheless, the GN was still an important military force, whose strength and armament far exceeded those of the FSLN. The Sandinista leaders were perfectly aware of the fact that even the slightest military setback could strengthen Somoza or at least allow the Americans to impose a solution to the conflict from which they would be excluded. They therefore decided to continue their offensive.

The Northern Front on the Offensive

The Northern Front, under the command of Germán Pomares, launched its next attack on 26 March with the capture of the city of El Jícaro in Nueva Segovia province by the column Óscar Turcios. The guerrillas also managed to lure reinforcements sent by the GN

to support the defeated forces in El Jícaro into several ambushes. Through these diversions, the Sandinista leaders turned south to prevent the GN from concentrating its forces against Pomares.

At this stage of operations, their planning still did not provide for an insurrection in Estelí: only for a combined action of the forces led by Elías Noguera and Cristhian Pichardo in the Condega area. For this, the column of Salvador Loza had to position itself between Estelí and Condega to contain GN reinforcements. There, the guerrillas shot down two aircraft, including one O-2A, but in the course of their subsequent retreat they ended up fighting practically inside Estelí. The column General Pedro Altamirano, meanwhile, attacked El Sauce, where it shot down another aircraft.

Meanwhile, other units launched diversionary attacks on the towns of Achuapa, Rio Grande, San Rafael del Norte, Pueblo Nuevo and

During fighting in the Estelí area and then inside the town in early 1979, the FSLN managed to capture a handful of Staghounds. At least one of these was promptly turned against its former owners – now clearly marked as operated by the insurgency – as visible in this photograph from the period. (Pit Weinert Collection)

Wreckage of an FAN O-2A '316', one of at least two aircraft of this type that were shot down by the FSLN in early 1979. (Pit Weinert Collection)

In nearly every GN base that was overrun by the FSLN, the insurgents found a significant amount of abandoned – often sabotaged – vehicles. This scene shows a mix of diverse jeeps, US and German-made trucks, and also one of the rare Nicaraguan M3 half-tracks. (via David François)

Wreckage of a C-47 shot down by the insurgency somewhere in the Condega-Cucali area in March 1979. The aircraft had the serial number 411. (FSLN release)

action, the urban units entered the battle, thus springing the second insurrection of Estelí – without this ever being planned by their own leaders.[245]

Indeed, the Sandinistas led by Francisco Rivera were left with no choice but to enter Estelí on 8 April, not for military but essentially political reasons. The GN, which learned the lessons of the September uprising, had dispersed its forces throughout the city, making progress particularly difficult. While trying to lessen pressure upon Pomares' forces, about 400 insurgents became involved in one of the fiercest battles of the entire war, and certainly since September 1978. Their energetic action initially proved successful.[246] However, because their operation was not coordinated with other parts of the FSLN, and because the insurgency outside Estelí had meanwhile decided to abandon control of the Pan-American Highway, after a week of intensive fighting they found themselves in a difficult position. The column Filemón Rivera found itself scattered between San Rafael del Norte, San Sebastián de Yalí, El Sauce and San Juan de Limay. Other units had the task of harassing and ambushing the road that led from Estelí to Condega, preventing GN forces from Somoto, Ocotal or elsewhere from moving towards Estelí from the north. Another part of the guerrilla remained mobile between Estelí, La Concordia and

Limay, forcing the GN to dissipate its forces. For the Sandinistas, the main danger came from the possibility of the GN bringing in a large concentration of troops from Managua by the Pan-American Highway. It therefore appeared necessary to take control of this road and thus cut off Estelí. At this point, the mere presence of an insurgency in the proximity of the town caused an uprising in it: eager to take part in the

San Rafael. However, and despite their best efforts, the insurgents failed to concentrate their forces in Estelí and thus lost the town again.[247]

Despite this setback, fighting erupted in the neighbouring towns of Condega and Cucali, where the insurgents had managed to shoot down a C-47 transport and another Cessna O-2.[248] On 8 April, the combined Facundo Picado and César Augusto Salinas Pinell columns attacked Condega. Further south, the guerrillas faced the GN in the western suburbs of Managua and León. Pomares attacked Yalí and burned the GN HQ in order to relieve pressure on the forces of Rivera in Estelí. The latter, with some of his troops, then abandoned the city and went to Jinotega, leaving 400 of his men around Estelí to repel a possible GN attack when Somoza sent about 2,500 soldiers, including elite units, to take back the town.[249]

On the Atlantic coast, to relieve the Somozist pressure on Estelí, the column Jacinto Hernández left the old Spanish fortress of Inmaculada Concepción, on the banks of the Rio San Juan, heading towards Nueva-Guinea. Its mission was to distract the GN forces and provide a supply line from the San Juan River, then to walk to the Chontales department and finally to Managua. It had to distract the enemy while conditions were set up in the rest of the country such that, once the GN dispersed, insurrections were possible in the cities. The unrest in the cities would also prevent the GN from concentrating all its military strength where the guerrilla columns were. The GN was thus in a no-win situation. If it left the cities, urban agitation increased; but if it stayed in the cities, the movement of guerrilla columns was facilitated.

As fighting continued in the north, the FSLN began hostilities in the south in April near the Costa Rican border. Skirmishes took place in Rivas, Cárdenas, Colon, Orosí and Sapoá. Guerrillas erected roadblocks in the Managua region. In Masaya, the combat unit Pedro Arauz Palacios launched a violent attack against the city of Catarina about 30km south of the capital.[250] These actions were all aimed to ease the pressure against the guerrillas engaged in the battle for Estelí in the north but also to prevent the sending of reinforcement to the south. On 3 May, the Sandinistas attacked a GN post at La Concepción in Masaya province. A week later, a larger force raided a barracks in the city of Santa Teresa, in Carazo province, 50 km south of Managua.[251]

The GN General Staff decided to abandon the Estelí headquarters and consolidate its forces further south. With 1,500 soldiers, from 4-10 May, the military encircled the plains surrounding Nueva-Guinea near the Atlantic coast, in which the column Jacinto Hernández made the mistake of entering. Perceiving the danger, the Sandinista leadership asked Pomares and Rivera to regroup their forces to manoeuvre towards Managua with the immediate objective of relieving the surrounded column Jacinto Hernández. However, it was too late: supported by attack aircraft and helicopters, the GN quickly knocked out the staff of this column – including Iván Montenegro Báez, Óscar Benavides Lanuza and Adolfo García Barberena – while 125 fighters were killed while trying to break through along the Nueva-Guinea-El Rama-Managua axis. This action was the most serious defeat suffered by the FSLN during the 1979 offensive.

Despite the Nueva-Guinea defeat, the Sandinistas maintained their

An M4 Sherman attempts to cross a barricade consisting of paving stones, like those erected by the locals in Jinotega in May 1979. (Albert Grandolini Collection)

Wreck of the second O-2A shot down by the FSLN in early 1979. (via Tom Cooper)

pressure. In mid-May, fighting continued along the Rio Guasaule on the border with Honduras, but also around the villages of Wiwilí in Nueva Segovia province, Ciudad Rama in Zelaya, Juigalpa in Chontales and Morrito in Rio San Juan.[252] In the Matagalpa region, the Crescencio Rosales combat unit carried out numerous actions, including the capture of the San Ramón garrison. It also launched an assault on San Dionisio on 9 May, killing or wounding eight GN.[253]

On 17 May, Pomares and his 600 fighters encircled and seized the city of Jinotega. The population supported the Sandinistas by raising barricades, but few joined the fighters. After bloody confrontations that lasted two days, the GN regained control of the city and pursued the guerrillas in the surrounding hills, while Pomares was wounded before dying on 24 May. The columns that fought at Jinotega then went in the direction of Matagalpa to join the Rosales Crescencio column at Puertas Viejas. They collided there with a column of 300 GN with vehicles and a tank. The soldiers were supported by artillery and a 'push and pull' jet. The fighting lasted nearly four days before the GN withdrew.[254]

In Estelí, the GN set up a double encirclement of the city with reinforcements coming from the Pan-American road. Only the use of aviation, armoured vehicles, airborne troops and important ground reinforcements forced the guerrillas to leave the city and take refuge in the nearby mountains. Sandinista forces evacuated Estelí in good order from the south and caused heavy GN losses, including

35 soldiers who were killed in Cucamonga. This demonstrated that thousands of soldiers were now unable to beat a column of fewer than 200 guerrillas.[255] On 27 May, the 52nd anniversary of the founding of the GN, the FSLN launched strong attacks against Managua, León and Jinotega.

The FSLN's National Directorate in Palo Alto realized that despite their successes, the offensive was developing without much coordination. The destroyed Jacinto Hernández column was originally planned to form the eastern flank of the Southern Front, preventing the GN from taking action to support the military in the north when Pomares seized

Cheerful insurgents atop the M4A3 Sherman captured during their assault on El Naranjo. (via Mark Lepko)

Jinotega. With the Sandinistas thus proving unable to curb the GN's manoeuvring abilities, the National Directorate was left with no choice but to accelerate the entry into action of the Southern Front. Furthermore, it opened the Central Front with an insurrection in Managua, aimed at supporting its decisive operations in the south.

The difficulties of the offensive revived the divisions within the FSLN. The GPP and the Proletarians Tendencies criticized the Tercerists' strategy and asked to delay the general insurrection which was to start on 4 June. The Tercerists wanted instead to accelerate the offensive to prevent the GN from taking the initiative. Finally, recognizing that this would be the final offensive the FSLN would be able to support with all available means, Tomás Borge and Jaime Wheelock – who represented the GPP and the Proletarians Tendencies – agreed to follow the Tercerist idea. For them, it was imperative to coordinate the offensive on all fronts in time and space – especially because the Southern Front could no longer operate out of Costa Rica due to diplomatic pressure.

Southern Front

Despite the FSLN's bold military actions since 1977, the GN retained its military capacity and manoeuvring power in the spring of 1979, which enabled it to concentrate its forces on each insurrection, first against one city and then against another. Indeed, at the beginning of the 1979 offensive, despite the setbacks suffered by its troops in various battlefields, the dictatorship still had the power to strike hard against its adversaries, as shown by the operation perpetrated on 16 April 1979 at the Reparto Veracruz in León, where the main leader of the Western Front, Cristián Pérez, was killed on 12 May, and then the Jacinto Hernández column destroyed five days later. It was obvious in these circumstances that different insurgent fronts were experiencing growing difficulties in coordinating their operations, and lacked not only the firepower of the GN but also the ability to counter them. Nevertheless, the FSLN was beyond the point at which it could retreat: many of its units were forced into a positional warfare in order to enable others to retreat and regroup, or manoeuvre and return for a counterattack. The insurgency was thus left with no choice: if it did not strike the final blow against the government it would lose the war

A still from a video showing GN troops in the process of forming in the village of El Ostional, before their counterattack. Note their new ballistic helmets, flak vests and Galil assault rifles. (via Mark Lepko)

and face the consequences.

The crucial role was now to be played by the Southern Front, which was certainly the best-armed, best-trained and best-organized of all of the FSLN's elements, and commanded by Edén Pastora. He had about 600 combatants in total, organized into the columns Ricardo Salinas Talavera, Óscar Pérez Cassar and Eduardo Contreras Escobar, commanded respectively by Alvaro Ferrey, Alvaro Diroy Mendez and Javier Pichardo. They entered Nicaragua in March, through the Rivas department. Headed by Benedicto Menses, the Iván Montenegro column acted as the rear-guard, while in the lead the units deployed for attack in two directions: an assault on the town of Rivas, led by Commander Alvaro Diroy Mendez, and an advance on El Naranjo and Hill 155, and then along the axis Ostional-San Juan del Sur-Rivas.[256]

At dawn on 25 May, the 46 fighters of column Francisco Gutiérrez entered the department of Rivas with the mission to take the Pan-American Highway and carry out harassment actions in and around the city of Rivas. Three days later, on the morning of 28 May, column

Ricardo Talavera attacked the GN at El Naranjo and seized Hill 155 after heavy fighting. Somoza sent large GN contingents to a village near El Ostional, but to no avail: on 29 May, column Francisco Gutiérrez was already inside Rivas.[257]

The local GN commander, Colonel Alesio Gutiérrez, and his deputy, Captain Sacasa, reacted by deploying Staghound armoured cars supported by EEBI elite troops. However, their counterattack was beaten back with some loss, and thus the government lost control over the entire district of La Puebla and El Palenque district up to the International School of Agriculture.

To add salt to the injury, on the same day the column Eduardo Contreras seized the GN barracks in El Naranjo, where in the course of 48 hours of fighting, the government lost over 100 troops, one M4A3 Sherman and one of its precious aircraft. Worse still, the insurgents also captured hundreds of firearms and extensive stocks of ammunition.

Battle for Hill 155

Clashes between Sandinistas and the GN were also taking place in other villages in the Rivas department, such as Las Mancuernas or Peñas Blancas. Pastora, who had installed his command post between El Naranjo and Los Mojones, was faced by Colonel Pablo Emilio Salazar Paíz, known as 'Commander Bravo', a brilliant and courageous GN officer who was assigned to defend the isthmus of Rivas, the shores of Lake Nicaragua and especially the Pan-American Highway. He had to create a solid defensive buffer to prevent the advance of the Southern Front. On 1 June 1979, the GN unleashed its counteroffensive by attacking El Naranjo and Hill 155. Its infantry was supported by artillery pieces mounted on Mamenic Line boats and patrol boats from Salinas Bay equipped with 150mm howitzers. The GN and the FAN hit with full force: the O-2s and the single Arava pounded the Sandinistas with rockets and strafed them, while the T-33s and C-47s began deploying US-made Mk.82 250kg bombs. The longer the battle went on, the more artillery the GN brought in: it eventually deployed a large concentration of 81mm, and 120mm mortars, several recoilless 57mm guns and Argentina-made Yararà III multiple rocket launchers, equipped to fire Albatros 70mm artillery rockets – adapted by Israeli advisors to be carried on US-made 4WDs near the 'Bunker' of the Loma de Tiscapa. The unit deploying all these artillery pieces was commanded by Colonel Enrique Jacobi. With its arrival, the fighting in southern Nicaragua reached the dimensions of a classic, 'conventional' war.[258]

Luckily for the Nicaraguan population, the battle for Hill 155 took place in sparsely inhabited territory. With the exception of Rivas there were no large urban areas: the landscape was dominated by hills, pastures, mountains and rivers, with the vastness of the great Cocibolca lake to the east. Peñas Blancas and Sapoá had been emptied of their inhabitants. The struggle here was not that of the 'militia on the barricades' as in the bigger towns further north, but a classic war with trenches, casemates, mines and barbed wire. The 600 insurgents – the best the FSLN could offer – armed with FN FALs, were facing nearly 3,000 EEBI troops – the best Somoza had – armed with Galil assault rifles and supported by several groups of foreign mercenary and advisors.[259]

Intense fighting lasted 13 days, by day and night, including continuous artillery barrages or air strikes, turning the Southern Front into the main theatre of the war. The fight for Hill 155 turned into one of the bloodiest battles of the entire war, and certainly of the Southern Front, yet still the government forces failed in their task. The column Eduardo Contreras led by Javier Pichardo held out at Hill 155, withstanding no less than 27 infantry attacks. One of the factors

EEBI troops and one of their Staghounds during fighting in the Rivas department in June 1979. (via Mark Lepko)

A CH-34 of the FAN while carrying reinforcements for the battle for Hill 155 in early June 1979. (via Mark Lepko)

The appearance of RPG-7s within the ranks of FSLN insurgents in June 1979 was the virtual 'nail in the coffin' for the GN: their availability made most armoured vehicles highly vulnerable to insurgent infantry. (via David François)

strongly influencing the outcome was that the Sandinista National Directorate – aware of the crucial moment, and that the Southern Front was tying down the bulk of the GN – did its best to reinforce its involved units with artillery and modern infantry weapons. It deployed small units equipped with 82mm mortars and 75mm cannons, Soviet-designed ZPU machine guns acquired from Czechoslovakia and RPG-seven rocket launchers. It also did its best to recruit additional troops and rush them through training centres along the border with Costa Rica. The Southern Front eventually ended the battle reinforced instead of weakened, with about 900 combatants by mid-June 1979.

Another reason the FSLN leaders invested so heavily in the south was their fear that otherwise the GN might not only defeat its best troops, but subsequently also turn north and defeat several other insurgent

The aftermath of an air strike flown either by T-33s or C-47s: a crater of a US-made Mk.82 250kg bomb. (via David François)

The final insurrection saw widespread involvement of civilian activists. This group of girls is throwing glass bottles on the road in an attempt to make it impassable for GN vehicles. (via Mark Lepko)

One of the Argentina-made Yarará III multiple rocket launchers equipped to fire 70mm rockets, adapted by Israeli advisors on a US-made 4WD chassis, in action in May-June 1979. (Albert Grandolini Collection)

units, one after the other. In an attempt to relieve the Southern Front, the Sandinista leadership unleashed urban insurrections throughout the country. Meanwhile, the forces of the guerrilla columns were dispersed in their retreats, such as the Pablo Úbeda column which was still in the mountainous area of the north, recovering from earlier fighting. The Northern Front was also completely exhausted, in the process of recruiting hundreds of new combatants, who all required time to be organized and trained. Thus, neither could play a lead role in this effort. [260] The urban guerrillas therefore had to lead the final assault – and this simultaneously, in the north, west and south – while regular insurgent units were only to play a supportive role by distracting the government and cutting off communications between Managua and Masaya, Granada and Carazo.

Start of the Insurrection

Tomás Borge and Humberto Ortega officially announced the beginning of the insurrection via Radio Sandino, called for a total mobilization of Sandinista forces on 4 June, while the FPN, FAO and MPU called for a national strike.[261] In addition to the organization of the strike, the civil organizations were also charged with setting up the structures necessary for the continuation of the war: underground hospitals, supplies for fighters, training the population in first aid and organization of a civil defence. The general strike was only the prelude to the insurgency that set cities in the Pacific region, the political and economic heart of Nicaragua, ablaze.[262] The objective was to disperse GN forces without giving them the opportunity to regroup and to attack Pastora's forces in the south.

The Western Front operated in the north-western region of the country, around Chinandega, Chichigalpa, El Viejo and Corinto. The plan was to take control of the garrisons of Chichigalpa and Ingenio San Antonio to seize weapons and encircle Chinandega, the largest city in the region.[263] For this, the GPP Tendency had four well-trained and disciplined combat units in Chinandega, Corinto and El Viejo, but they were poorly armed. The Sandinistas could also rely on Proletarian units which were well established in the working areas of Corinto and Ingenio San Antonio. These units were intended to distract, harass and provoke insurrection while the well-armed and structured forces of the Tercerists intervened. A force of 60-100 men with heavy weapons advanced on the Potosi-El Viejo-Chinandega axis, while a unit of about 40 guerrillas from Honduras passed through Rancheria to attack Chinandega. A final Tercerist unit commanded by Sergio Mendoza also came from Honduras to attack Somotillo, Villanueva and then Chinandega.[264]

In Chichigalpa, on 21 May, FSLN fighters attacked the commando of the town of Posoltega. On the 25th, the GN retaliated by taking the town of Chichigalpa, killing eight people and forcing the fighters

to flee to El Chonco. In Chinandega, the plan of insurrection was to cover the town with barricades until a guerrilla column arrived. On 2 June, Chinandega fighters gathered in different parts of the town, but the group of Tercerist militants was discovered by the GN, triggering the infamous massacre of El Calvarío. The commander of the Tercerist troops was killed that day as the insurgency attempt was crushed by the GN, which surrounded the town, causing the departure of all organized Sandinista forces.

A guerrilla column of about 40 fighters entered Nicaragua via Somotillo and reached Ranchería, where it learnt about the Chinandega massacre and the failure of the insurrection. It tried to regroup the fighters who fled the city for the hills around El Viejo and the foothills of El Chonco volcano. The GN attacks were halted but the Sandinistas failed to invest Chinandega. The GN had dispersed its forces in the outskirts of the city, fortifying the tallest buildings. To force GN troops to withdraw, the FSLN organized an ambush involving 300 people at San Benito between Chichigalpa and Chinandega. Of a GN detachment which included troops from the CONDECA with armoured vehicles, supported by T-33 jets, 20 GN were killed and the guerrillas seized a tank. The GN withdrew and constructed positions on some minor heights towards Chinandega, where they started a fight of position.

Meanwhile, a column headed by Sergio Mendoza entered Nicaragua to seize towns north of Chinandega: Somotillo, Santo Tomás, San

The sole FAN Arava light transport in action while pressed into service as a light striker in June 1979. Note the 'bulbs' containing Browning machine guns on each side of the forward fuselage. (Courtesy La Prensa)

Insurgents armed with a mix of hunting rifles and FN FALs on the streets of León in June 1979. (via David François)

Insurgents in León arming (or rearming) themselves with Galil assault rifles captured from the GN. (via David François)

Francisco, Cinco Pinos, San Pedro del Norte and Villanueva. This column, which belonged to the Proletarian Tendency, was made up of 35 fighters who could not enter Nicaragua until the third week of June. They had G3 rifles, HK-21 machine guns, 81mm mortars and 75mm recoilless guns acquired in Portugal. The GN blocked them in Cerro Partido, starting a series of violent battles and a war of position in the middle of the canyons and hills that lasted for 15 days. The Sandinistas then attacked the GN from the rear and seized Villa Salvadorita on 15 July. The GN counterattacked with CONDECA forces and took over Villanueva. The FSLN needed reinforcements from León to continue its advance, but with the announcement of the departure of Somoza the GN withdrew.[265]

After the ambush of San Benito, the Sandinistas decided to seize the Chichigalpa HQ after taking that of Ingenio San Antonio. The attack on Chichigalpa prompted the GN in Chinandega to send 200 soldiers as reinforcements, but these troops fell into an ambush on 20 June, when the Sandinistas recovered a tank in good condition, along with 50 machine guns and rifles. On the 24th, Chichigalpa was taken. As a result of these operations, guerrillas attacked Corinto. On 18 July, following the announcement of the departure of Somoza, the Chinandega garrison laid down its arms after blowing up the HQ, where there were many prisoners. If the operations in Chinandega department proved more difficult than expected, the FSLN's strategic objective was nonetheless achieved since the insurgency in the region prevented the military from sending troops to the second largest city in the country, León, where an insurrection broke out on 7 June.[266]

Insurrection in León

In León, the Eastern Front's offensive plan consisted of simultaneously attacking the GN's support points, including their HQ, the prison, central bank and Godoy airport, which concentrated around 600 soldiers. At the same time, the possible arrival of GN reinforcements was contained by organizing ambushes on the main accesses to the city. The battle for León would last nearly three weeks.

The GPP Tendency had six combat units in León. Coordinating with the Tercerists, three units prevented GN reinforcements while the others attacked the prison and the HQ. A combat unit was set up in Quezalguaque to prevent GN reinforcements from coming to Chinandega. On 7 June, it faced a military contingent with armoured vehicles and planes. Some of the GN crossed the Sandinista lines, but a reinforcing unit managed to block them. Another ambush was placed at La Cartonera on the San Isidro-Telica road, where very violent fighting took place with a GN and CONDECA contingent from Guasaule. Another ambush was placed in Pancorva, in front of the bridge of La Leóna, to stop reinforcements coming from Managua. However, a GN contingent from La Lena – including numerous Staghound armoured cars – attempted to break through, and some

of its vehicles managed to do so before the fighting began in earnest.

In León, the FSLN first took care to secure the local prison, before continuing its advance into the town and then – with help of the populace – the local airport. Plenty of volunteers joined the movement and thanks to the capture of significant amounts of firearms, several new units were quickly established. However, on 16 June, General Gonzalo Evertz, commander of the GN in León, and some soldiers, protected by civilian hostages, managed to leave the HQ and take refuge in Fort Acosasco, about 12km outside but dominating the town, thus reinforcing the local garrison of about 150. Simultaneously, the FAN heavily bombed León in support of a small group of troops led by General Ariel Argüello Vale, left behind to guard the HQ. Eventually the situation forced the Sandinistas to concentrate on besieging Fort Acosasco, leaving behind only small units to guard the entrances to León.[267]

The final attack against the HQ began on 20 June with a shot from the captured M4 Sherman. The impact of the shell demoralized the defenders still inside: they all surrendered. However, the assault on Fort Acosasco proved far less effective, largely because FAN O-2s and T-33s subjected the insurgents to a series of vicious air strikes. The Sandinistas reacted by redeploying the sole Sherman to support their attack, in combination with one 57mm cannon. The FAS even deployed one of its makeshift bombers to attack the fortification – but without success: dozens of insurgents were then killed or wounded trying to assault it.

This vital installation only fell on the morning of 7 July, when General Evertz fled by helicopter, leaving the garrison behind. The last of the fort's defenders then attempted to break out, but ran into successive insurgent ambushes: at least 27 were killed and many others

Always enthusiastic about making use of captured armour, the FSLN was quick to turn an ex-GN Sherman against the defenders of Fort Acosasco on 6 and 7 July 1979. As usual, the vehicle promptly received numerous new 'service titles' sprayed around the hull. (FSLN release)

The final act of the drama in León began when the commander of the local garrison, General Gonzalo Evertz, fled from Fort Acosasco on board a FAN helicopter. (via David François)

disappeared, while only a handful were captured. The red and black flag of the Sandinistas was then finally hoisted over Fort Acosasco.[268]

Elsewhere in the León region, the Sandinistas took control of the town of El Sauce on 12 July and ambushed a GN convoy on the La Paz-Managua-León road. In El Sauce, the leader of about 140 FSLN insurgents negotiated with the commander of the 94-strong GN garrison, who were keen to surrender but were forced to fight under threats from another officer. There was no option but to storm the town; nearly a third of the garrison died fighting for a lost cause in a battle that lasted 36 hours.

Push in the North, the South-East and the Atlantic Coast

The outbreak of the insurgency didn't end the actions of the guerrillas. In the Northern Front, during a meeting in early June, Francisco Rivera reported that he received a letter from Julio Ramos to concentrate GPP forces in the Colonel Santos López Brigade in order to seize small towns, and finally Estelí. Rivera opposed it for lack of time and because of the dispersion of forces between those heading towards Estelí and others to Matagalpa. For the insurgency, the Northern Front had 12 columns dominated by the Tercerists and the GPP, some of them composed of several squads or combat groups.[269]

Rivera moved part of his troop, a little more than 400 men, to join the column Óscar Turcios commanded by Javier Carrión, who replaced Germán Pomares. The forces of Rivera and Carrión had to be released to prepare for the capture of Estelí and Matagalpa. The column Pedro Altamirano, with 120 men, seized San Rafael del Norte and fought towards Yali, which it left for Estelí with 340 fighters. As the columns prepared to march on Matagalpa, the GPP Tendency, led by Bayardo Arce, sent his fighters to reinforce the attacks on Nueva Segovia and Madriz.

Rivera arrived in Estelí on 9 June at the head of eight columns of the Northern Front, including those of Bonifacio Montoya and César Augusto Salinas. The city had been largely destroyed by GN aerial bombing during the April uprising. As soon as the guerrillas entered, the fighting began. In a direct confrontation with the GN, many were wounded.[270] Column Donoso Zeledón entered the city, then other guerrilla columns joined the battle. The GN was strategically located in the highest buildings of Estelí – in banks, the Telcor building, the Cathedral and colleges – its firepower reinforced by artillery, a Sherman tank and two armoured vehicles. There were about 300 guerrillas, only a quarter of whom had modern weapons, the others having hunting rifles and small arms. The column commanded by Julio Ramos entered the city on 20 June, followed by that of Omar Cabezas and then the brigade Colonel Santos López, commanded by Omar Halleslevens and Cristhian Pichardo. The fighting was fierce, but on 2 July GN troops regrouped in the central garrison, leaving the rest of the city in the hands of the Sandinistas. Estelí, however, was regularly bombed by the FAN and pounded by garrison mortars for several days longer.[271]

The siege of the garrison lasted 12 days. The GN, commanded by Vicente Zúñiga, was well entrenched and maintained a corridor between the garrison and the airstrip under its control, allowing it to receive equipment and supplies. Finally, on 16 July, a Sandinista civilian aircraft dropped four homemade bombs on the garrison, while a handmade 75mm gun fired seven shots at the fortress, breaching its thick walls in several places. The insurgents deployed bulldozers to widen the gaps and thus managed to enter and successfully assault the fort.[272]

In Matagalpa, the insurrection began on 4 July and the Sandinistas quickly besieged the 200 soldiers in the garrison. Matagalpa was then a town with very particular characteristics, completely surrounded by hills. The GN held the cathedral, the Eliseo Picado Institute (in the upper part of the town) and the Cerro La Virgen. It even managed to launch a counterattack towards the Cerro de Apante sector. Javier Carríon and Bayardo Arce led the Sandinista forces, which were composed of the Crescencio Rosales, Salvador Amador and Carlos Arroyo Pineda combat units, as well as columns General Pedro Altamirano, Óscar Turcios and Escuadra Héroes y Mártires de Veracruz. The fighting for control of the city was violent, especially on the El Calvarío hill and Cerro La Virgen. Finally, on 15 July, with the help of an armoured vehicle taken from the GN, the Sandinistas seized the hospital, the last position held by the GN.[273]

After four months of a tenacious offensive, the Northern Front had liberated Estelí, Nueva Segovia, Madriz, Matagalpa and Jinotega departments. More than 20 towns and villages were under Sandinista

During the fighting for Matagalpa, the insurgents captured at least one Staghound. Although lacking both front fenders, this vehicle was promptly deployed to fight the GN. (Pit Weinert Collection)

Fighting in Matagalpa caused heavy suffering for the local population. This pair of Red Cross workers are trying to remove an injured woman from the street. (Albert Grandolini Collection)

This is probably the same vehicle, perhaps after the war. Note that instead of the title FSLN being sprayed around the hull, it wore the FSLN flag on the glacis plate as a method of identification. (Pit Weinert Collection)

control, including the three crossings on the Honduran border and the strategic city of Sebaco on the Pan American Highway between Managua and Estelí.[274] On 11 July, Northern Front units were less than 25km from Managua and there was fighting on the outskirts of the capital in the villages of Tipitapa and Sabana Grande.

There was also guerrilla warfare in the rest of the country. East of Lake Nicaragua, in the Chontales area, a column commanded by Luis Carrión began its march on Managua, while skirmishes took place in La Pimienta and Morillo in Rio San Juan department.

In the north-east of the country, in the Zelaya province bordering the Caribbean coast, the North-Eastern Front of Pablo Úbeda went on the offensive on 28 May. There were clashes in Puerto Cabeza on 15 July, along with Waslala, Prinzapolka and Siuna, while small FSLN units seized the mining towns of Bonanza and Rosita.[275] GN forces either surrendered or fled to Honduras. On 19 July, FSLN fighters reached the Coco River that forms the border with Honduras. The port of Bluefield was taken by men of the Simón Bolívar Brigade.

Fighting for Masaya

With the beginning of the general strike in early June, there was also action involving the Central Front, focusing on Managua and the Masaya region. In the latter, the plan for the insurgency was to attack Masaya and Ticuantepe at the same time and to establish an ambush to contain the reinforcements that would surely come from Managua. The FSLN's attack on Diriá, Diríomo and Catarina and the uprising of Granada prevented reinforcements from the south going to the city. Tercerist leader Hilarío Sánchez operated in the Masaya zone to cut GN communications between Managua and Commander Bravo in the south. He also launched an insurgency in Jinotepe, Diriamba and Diríomo, and on 6 June fighting finally began in Masaya.

The local insurgency was concentrated around the TCU Rufo Marin, including 250-300 combatants armed with up to 200 assault rifles, between 60 and 80 rifles and pistols, two RPG-7s, a light machine gun and one German-made MG-42 machine gun. Despite their reasonably good armament, the insurgents quickly suffered several severe blows. Eleven out of 16 members of this unit in La Reforma were killed during the first day of action. Then an attack on Ticuantepe failed because the local GN garrison was significantly reinforced and the assailants subsequently found themselves exposed to air strikes, which also caused heavy losses. By the third day of the insurgency, 8 June, the military was reinforced by the arrival of at least one Staghound, which eventually forced the Sandinistas to abandon their attack on the local HQ. Worse still, on 9 June a contingent of CONDECA troops arrived in Masaya and the insurgents realised their position was hopeless, retreating into the countryside to the south.[276]

The simultaneous insurrection in Managua forced the GN to withdraw its troops from the Masaya area. Three columns of insurgents therefore returned to the town and established control of most of it by 11 June: a day later, the local garrison was besieged. After nearly two weeks of continued assaults, the commander of the GN in Masaya, General Fermin Meneses, ordered his troops to take local civilians as hostages. Shielded by these, the troops left their barracks for Fort El Coyotepe on 24 June. While the government thus finally lost control over Masaya, it continued pounding the town with 120mm mortars and repeated air strikes for several more days.[277]

Managua Insurrection

At the beginning of June, the GN intensified its surveillance in Managua. The general strike in the capital was transformed into more violent demonstrations that turned into armed clashes. The FSLN planned for the uprising in the capital to begin a few days after the start of the strike, but events were rushed because of the actions of the

Dozens of German-made MG-42 machine guns were captured by the FSLN quite early during its final offensive, and pressed into service against government forces. (via David François)

The insurrection in the Managua area is probably the best documented part of the final insurgent push against the Somoza dictatorship. The involved 'muchachos' – as they were colloquially known by each other and the public – belonged to several columns of urban guerrillas, and thus rarely wore military fatigues. (via Mark Lepko)

population and its erecting of the first barricades.[278]

The Central Front therefore decided to launch the fight in Managua. The goal was to immobilize some GN forces and await the arrival of guerrilla columns to take the capital. The tactics adopted were essentially defensive, with the aim of annoying the enemy as much as possible, disperse government forces all over the city. The supreme command in the capital was composed of Joaquín Cuadra, Carlos Núñez, William Ramírez and Walter Ferreti, while the command of operations was entrusted to Raúl Venerío, Mónica Baltodano and Osbaldo Lacayo.

The Central Front knew that it could not afford to take control of the whole of Managua straight away. It therefore determined main and secondary battle zones in order to disperse the GN as much as possible, taking advantage of the city's geography. The channels running east of Managua represented a natural barrier that the FSLN used for defensive purposes. The main combat zone was the eastern part of the capital and part of the northern highway.[279] The command set the points where armed groups and trenches were to be placed to prevent the movement of soldiers. On bridges and crossing points, M-30 or MG-42 machine guns, fortified barricades, bazookas and at least one combat unit were placed to repel GN attacks.[280] In the secondary combat zones - the rest of the city - there was no definite front but instead mobile armed units adopted tactics of harassment.[281] In Managua, the FSLN had five RPG-2s with five rockets each, three .30-calibre machine guns, two MAC machine guns and some Garand and FAL rifles, the rest of its weaponry consisting of rifles, semi-automatic rifles, revolvers and homemade bombs.[282]

The uprising began on 9 June, with the Central Front ordered to remain in Managua for at least three days. The uprising started in the Nicarao, Central America and Acahualinca neighbourhoods. On 10 June, GN troops were fully dispersed, the west and east of the capital being in the hands of the population, backed by the Sandinistas and about 500 fighters of the Popular Militia,[283] with barricades erected, trenches dug and supply networks installed. The Central Front leadership based itself in the district of El Dorado,[284] while the San Cristobal Bridge, a strategic point, was defended by a fortified barricade with a .30-calibre machine gun and regular Sandinista units. The Sandinistas also managed to block the road that led to the international airport, La Mercedes, south of Managua and engaged in fierce fighting within 2km of the Bunker, the Somoza HQ.

During the 12th, about 3,000 GN[285] attacked with armoured vehicles, mortars and aviation support to break the defensive cordon of the eastern quarters established by the FSLN, while snipers harassed Sandinista positions. The fighting was intensifying and thousands of refugees received help from the Red Cross. Air and artillery attacks were systematic, causing death and destruction. Behind barricades and in trenches, militiamen with small-calibre weapons held their positions. The GN first concentrated its attacks to seize the canals in the district of El Riguero, defended only by militiamen. Four days after the beginning of the uprising, the Sandinistas still controlled the entire city with the exception of some residential neighbourhoods and part of the northern road from Portezuelo.[286]

On 14 June, the GN command decided to concentrate its efforts in Managua with the elite troops of the EEBI. GN reinforcements intended for Masaya were also diverted towards the capital, where the fighting intensified. More than 1,000 GN were involved in clean-up operations in the capital. Thus, the objective of the FSLN, which was to fix for a time the attention of Somoza's General Staff elsewhere other than on the Southern or Northern Front, was realized.

The GN began an operation of systematic reconquest of the capital by beginning to eliminate the weakest pockets of resistance. Tank and aviation forces were initially used in the western neighbourhood which suffered particularly. On 13 June, at the same time as it launched attacks in the western zone, the GN intensified its attempts to isolate the eastern zone. The entire defensive line of the San Cristobal Bridge to the Transportes Modernos bypass was subjected to air bombing and mortar attacks, and then to infantry attacks in the afternoon. The goal was to isolate as much as possible of the eastern part of the rest of the city. The FSLN sought to ease the pressure by small offensive actions. At this point the 'Liebre' battalion came into action. This combat unit was composed of elite fighters with the best weapons: FAL rifles, Galils, bazookas, RPG-2s and mortars. Its mission was to support the units in the trenches that were under attack from the enemy offensive. The Liebre helped them by fast and violent commando operations, directed by Walter Ferreti and Carlos Salgado.[287]

On 14 June, the GN offensive expanded, mainly in the eastern zone, with the districts of San Judas and Open no.3 heavily bombarded. The pressure became more intense on San Cristobal Bridge and the northern route. The Central Front Command was aware that resistance would not be able to continue like this. It had launched its offensive with only 150 fighters, joined by a few hundred militiamen, and didn't have the enemy's weight of fire. Resistance in the western neighbourhoods declined, with some taken over by the GN.[288]

Once the clearing of the western neighbourhoods was completed, the GN reinforced the eastern area, where pressure was stronger due to it being isolated from the rest of the city. Barricades destroyed by the tanks were nevertheless rebuilt the next day, but the Central

Another group of urban insurgents in the Managua area in June 1979. Note that many of the combatants wore scarves in red and black – the colours of the FSLN – to hide their identity, but also as a means of easier identification in combat. (via Mark Lepko)

Front knew that guerrilla columns from outside would not come to rescue them and that time was playing against the insurgents. The GN increased the bombings, while using radio to frighten the inhabitants by announcing its victories, revealing the dates and times it would begin clearing the districts and calling on the inhabitants to abandon the Sandinistas.

On 17 June, enemy pressure increased on the positions at El Dorado and trenches were taken, but the FSLN defensive system held. The next day, the GN intensified its offensive and forced the Sandinista command to leave El Dorado for the church of Sagrada Familia and the Duciali district.[289] The depletion of FSLN forces became perceptible, caused by the fatigue of incessant fighting and lack of supplies. With the militia by now almost unarmed and without ammunition, the GN began to seize barricades more easily by concentrating its forces against vital targets. To ease the pressure, the leadership of the Central Front formed the column Óscar Pérez Cassar, which was to fulfil the same mission as La Liebre.[290] This column was composed of 42 fighters led by the commander known as 'Chombo', with Douglas Duarte Zeledón as second in command.[291]

The Central Front demanded ammunition from Commander Humberto Ortega, who decided to supply Managua by air. On the morning of 18 June, avoiding the radars of Las Mercedes airport, a Piper Navajo aircraft dropped a cargo of ammunition in the eastern area. On 20 June, the defenders suffered a heavy bombardment and constant harassment by the GN, which infiltrated through gaps in the defence. The Central Front decided to abandon the barricades and instead organize their defence in the houses, making the enemy approach more vulnerable to their fire. They also decided to launch assaults on areas where the GN had managed to infiltrate and to organize ambushes to slow the advance of the military.

On 21 June, the Sandinista forces, in particular the Óscar Pérez Cassar column, went on the attack. The offensive continued on the 22nd and ejected the GN out of the positions it had taken. Somoza's forces, however, launched counterattacks on the El Paradito bridge, with the support of an armoured vehicle, but were pushed back. Commander César Augusto Silva's men ambushed an EEBI convoy and captured two machines guns. The struggle had become a typical urban confrontation, with house-to-house fighting, particularly in the El Dorado district.[292]

On 23 June, GN helicopters hit the city with bombs of between 100lb and 500lb. As the fighting continued, the GN lost 25 men on the northern route and even more in El Dorado and Colonia Luis Somoza in house-to-house fighting. The following days were difficult for the Sandinistas, bombing by helicopters causing enormous damage, destroying houses and forcing the fighters into hiding. Terror spread among the inhabitants, whose exodus grew in numbers.

Manoeuvre on the Southern Front

On the Southern Front, Edén Pastora withdrew his forces from El Naranjo and Hill 155, the enemy having caused numerous casualties with massive use of artillery and aviation strikes during the many attempts to retake these positions. Nevertheless, after studying all available reports, the FSLN National Directorate ordered the columns to resume their offensive from 15 June at latest. For this purpose, numerous new units were hurriedly established, tending to be put under the command of those who had distinguished themselves in the battles of the previous two weeks – including Alejandro Guevara, Laureano Mairena Aragon, Carlos Duarte Tablada, Vladimir Andino, Orlando Aguilera, José Vargas and Ricardo Gutiérrez. The General Staff of the Front was also restructured, with Chief of Staff José Valdivia Hidalgo, Álvaro Ferrey Pernudi as Chief of Operations, Javier Pichardo Ramírez as Chief of Intelligence, Sebastián González as Chief of the Rearguard, Marío Avilés Sáenz in charge of manpower and Richard Lugo Kautz as Chief of Operations in Río San Juan.[293] With this reorganization, there was a qualitative and quantitative leap in the composition of the Southern Front.

On 15 June, the Somoza dictatorship still had troops in Peñas Blancas and Sapoá. The advance of the South-eastern Front to Rivas depended on the neutralisation of these strongholds, so the Southern Front staff was developing a plan to seize both cities using artillery, mortars and columns led by Laureano Mairena, Ricardo Vargas, Orlando Aguilera and Carlos Duarte. During this second phase of its offensive, the Southern Front greatly increased its firepower through the addition of further batteries equipped with 75mm guns and 82mm and 120mm mortars. These were deployed in combat for the first time during assaults on Peñas Blancas and Sapoá. The Southern Front was then further reinforced by the addition of Soviet-made ZPU-4 heavy machine guns, which had the nickname 'four mouths.' Their prompt entry into the battle was possible due to the arrival of a sizeable group of Chilean volunteers, all with military experience and having been trained in Cuba, plus several Cuban advisors.

Pastora deployed his six columns for simultaneous attacks on Peñas-Blancas and Sapoá, but also along the Pan-American Highway. The first into action was the column of Laureano Mairena Aragón, which advanced to the Ostayo River to organize an ambush on the road between Sapoá and La Virgen, thus containing any reinforcements. The column of Ricardo Vargas quickly accomplished its mission and secured Sapoá, while that of Orlando Aguilera attacked Peñas Blancas, only to find itself under intense artillery fire by the GN, forcing it to withdraw all the way back to Sapoá. Meanwhile, the rearguard established itself in a position on the heights of Las Vueltas, while other columns protected the command post, the artillery battalion and the medical post.[294]

Peñas Blancas was then an active border town with much commercial activity related to international transit, duty-free shops, warehouses and customs agencies. Given its location on the border with Costa Rica, it had already been the target of frequent attacks and harassment by the Sandinistas. The column of Bolivar Juárez – supported by a battery of five 75mm cannons – finally seized the city after a struggle of less than two hours. The commander of the local GN unit, Morales 'El Diablo', was captured.[295]

The GN commander of Peñas Blancas, Morales 'El Diablo', was captured by insurgents of the column Bolivar Juárez. (via David François)

Further west, around Cardenas and San Juan del Sur, in the sector of Sota Caballo to hills 106, 109 and the bridge of La Pita No. 1, advanced guerrilla columns had entered the El Aceituno sector. It was there that on 17 June, the GN stopped the advance of the Sandinista forces to the point that the fighting transformed into static, positional warfare. Little changed even when, on 13 July, the GN deployed reinforcements in this area; their attacks were all repelled by the guerrillas.

The popular uprising was also developing in the rest of the Rivas department. On 21 June, after 20 hours of fighting, the hacienda San Martín in Las Salinas, which the GN had transformed into a strategic location, fell. In Rivas, the GN barracks were attacked and the Sandinistas took control of the neighbourhoods of El Rastro, San Felix and El Palmar on 25 June. To neutralise the threat from GN reinforcements, the column Francisco Gutiérrez destroyed the bridge over the Gil González river. On 3 July, the city of Rivas was partially taken by the FSLN, but the fighting continued. Three days later, GN mortars targeted San José Hospital, massacring patients and medical staff. On 10 July, the FAS sent ammunition and supplies. The next day, one of its aircraft crashed in the region of La Chocolata after delivering its cargo to Rivas.

At the same time, the column Eduardo Contreras continued to fight in the area between La Virgen and Sapoa. On 13 July, it planned to conduct a tactical retreat in the vicinity of Rivas to the municipality of Tola, leaving the city of Belén. Airborne EEBI troops landed in Ingenio Dolores to retake Belén, where the guerrilla presence prevented reinforcements from being sent to Rivas. When the GN entered Belén, it engaged in a massacre of civilians on 15 July, while the other guerrilla columns of the Southern Front continued to support the war of position.[296]

At this time the Sandinistas controlled a logistics centre and staging area along the Nicaraguan border with Costa Rica, consisting of a corridor 25km long and some 3-8km wide around the Peñas-Blancas border post. This so-called 'liberated territory', which included the cities of Ostayo, Soticaballo, Sapoa, Tola, Nancimi, Belén and Potosi stretched from Salinas Bay on the Pacific to the city of Cardenas on the shores of Lake Nicaragua. An area of this corridor extended 15km north towards Rivas.[297] After a month of fighting, the GN was exhausted and on 18 July signs of disintegration appeared.

The Retreat from Managua

At the end of June, Managua was transformed into an insurrectional base in which Sandinista forces created complicated labyrinths of communication from one quarter to another, from house to house, digging tunnels to escape the enemy. But this desperate resistance could not last long given the increasing pressure from government troops. Therefore, on 27 June at 7:00 p.m., Central Front Command decided to proceed with an orderly retreat.[298]

The plan was to withdraw to Masaya, 30km from the capital, to consolidate the south-eastern zone, cut off the enemy supply and strengthen the Southern Front. The vanguard was led by commanders Joaquín Cuadra, William Ramírez and Raúl Venerío, the centre by commanders Núñez, Osbaldo Lacayo and Walter Ferrety, and the rearguard by commanders Baltodano, Marcos Somarriba, Ramón Cabrales and Rolando Orozco.[299] The retreat began on 27 June before dark. Initially it involved about 1,500 people, but soon there were about 6,000 people of Managua, including the young, women, children and dozens of injured, more than 20 in a serious condition. There were 1,500 in the vanguard, 2,500 in the centre and 2,000 in the rear-guard.[300]

Around 7:00 a.m. the vanguard ran into a GN patrol. Upon hearing shots, the bulk of the column began to scatter, and fighters had to use threats so the whole column didn't break up. Shortly after 9:00 a.m. the column was spotted by the GN and bombed by a T-33 jet, two helicopters and a DC-3, killing six combatants and wounding a further 16. The Sandinistas decided to stay hidden and didn't restart their advance until the following night. At 1:00 a.m. the column finally

Many days of fighting in the Managua area created immense problems for the local population, which found it increasingly hard to find food. This group of civilians was photographed while swarming a truck carrying food on one of the roads outside the city on 29 June 1979. (Mark Lepko Collection)

reached Nindirí, and an hour later arrived at the Salesian College of Masaya, tired and hungry. The arrival of the Managua forces made it possible to consolidate the defences of Masaya and Diriamba, and to cut the supply link of the Somoza forces in the south.[301]

Diplomatic Struggle

While the Somoza regime faced Sandinista attacks, the diplomatic situation was also turning against the regime. Mexico announced the breaking of diplomatic relations with Managua on 20 May.[302] Although Costa Rica had already broken relations with Nicaragua; Colombia, Panama and Venezuela, as well as the US, refused to follow the Mexican position. They wanted to protect Somoza's opponents who had taken refuge in their embassies in Managua, but also hoped to retain an influence over the crisis that was shaking the country. Nevertheless, international hostility against Somoza continued to grow, and when he asked the OAS to condemn Costa Rica for its complicity with the guerrillas, the organization rejected his request

The Carter administration intervened again to try to stem the Nicaraguan crisis. On 9 and 10 June, on the orders of the State Department, Ambassador William Bowdler travelled to Costa Rica and the Andean Pact countries to request their participation in finding a way out of the crisis.[303] But an OAS meeting in Washington rejected the Carter administration's proposal to send a peacekeeping force to Nicaragua.[304] Behind this rejection, it was difficult not to see the strong Latin American current linked to the international social democracy formed by Mexico, Panama, Venezuela, Costa Rica and the Dominican Republic which strongly rejected the idea of an American solution. Increasingly isolated, Somoza was unable to mobilize CONDECA military forces because of the problems that

the governments of El Salvador and Guatemala had with guerrillas in their countries. The only aid that Somoza could still benefit from, besides the usual substantial IMF funding, was arms deliveries from El Salvador and Israel.[305]

In Palo Alto, the FSLN leadership decided to reinforce its diplomatic offensive, mainly for fear of possible foreign intervention on Nicaraguan soil. It was looking for the formation of a Junta of National Reconstruction (JGRN) through meetings in San José between Violeta Barríos Chamorro, Tomás Borge and Humberto Ortega. On 17 June, the FSLN announced the composition of the JGRN, which included Violeta Barríos Chamorro, widow of the assassinated press boss, Sergio Ramírez Mercado of the *Los Doce* group, Alfonso Robelo Callejas, a businessman, Moises Hassan Morales, a university professor and GPP Tendency member, and Daniel Ortega of the Tercerists Tendency.[306] On the same day, Ecuador broke diplomatic relations with Somoza, while Andean Pact members declared a state of belligerence in Nicaragua, placing the Sandinistas and the Somoza regime on the same legal plane, a decision that provoked anger in Washington. The next day, Panama also broke relations with Somoza and recognized the JGRN.[307] The killing of US journalist Bill Stewart by GN soldiers on 20 June in front of television cameras provoked such a stir in the US that Washington decided to definitively end its ties with Somoza.[308]

While the US government rejected Somoza, it also wanted to limit FSLN power and retain the GN. William Bowdler insisted on the need for enlargement of the JGRN and the acceptance of a GN officer as the head of the military institution. Recently promoted general Federico Mejía was the candidate chosen by Somoza and American ambassador Lawrence Pezzullo to become the new leader of the GN.[309]

For his part, US Secretary of State Cyrus Vance proposed to the OAS measures to solve the crisis in Nicaragua: the replacement of Somoza by a transitional government, the establishment of a ceasefire, the sending of an inter-American peacekeeping force, stopping deliveries of weapons to belligerents and launching a programme of assistance and reconstruction. However, the resolution passed by the OAS on 23 June differed from Vance's proposals. The assembly wanted Somoza's departure and the installation of a government including all opposition forces, free elections, respect for human rights and humanitarian assistance.[310]

On 22 June, the US State Department accused Cuba of providing arms and military training to the Sandinista guerrillas, with weapons passing through Panama and Costa Rica. This was the first time the US administration had openly accused Havana of intervention in Nicaragua. This statement prompted fears of a possible US military intervention on the pretext of defending Central America against communist penetration. However, at the end of June, the Carter administration was still trying to find a peaceful solution to the conflict: it proposed that Somoza give up his power to a constitutional successor, who would form a Junta made up of people not linked to the old regime and to whom it would hand over his powers. This Junta would seek a ceasefire and form an interim government to prepare free elections to choose a new president.[311]

The new American ambassador to Managua, Lawrence Pezzullo, presented this plan to Somoza on 27 June. The dictator accepted it, but only on the condition that the Liberal Party and the GN retain their function during the transitional government period, a condition that was unacceptable to the opposition. Pezzullo tried without success to convince Somoza to change his position until mid-July.

On 28 June, Bowdler held secret talks in Panama with JGRN members, while on the 23rd and 24th, a FSLN representative had held meetings in Washington with the Assistant Secretary for Latin America and the new US ambassador in Managua.[312]

The fall of Jinotepe

As Washington began negotiations with the JGRN on 29 June, Sandinista forces that had withdrawn from Managua were resting at Masaya. The city, under the command of Hilarío Sanchez, was under fire from mortars in the fortress of El Coyotepe held by the GN, and remained under threat of an attack by the military. The Central Front Command decided to keep control of Masaya and liberate the entire department of Carazo to prevent communications to the south and isolated the GN's centre of operations in Granada.[313] This was achieved by taking Jinotepe. For this, the staff of Managua had troops evacuated from the capital formed into an impressive mobile force of eight platoons that became the Rolando Orozco battalion.[314]

Central Front took command of all forces in the south-east region and decided to strengthen the defence of Masaya. First aid clinics were set up, manufacture of small arms was organized, anti-aircraft shelters were consolidated, barricades and reinforced trenches expanded, and the cordon of defences extended in the outskirts of the city. The local command also requested the National Directorate to send equipment. The next day, a FAS plane landed on a stretch of the Masaya-Managua highway and unloaded FAL ammunition and bazooka rockets. Two days later, two more planes landed with further equipment.

The situation of the Sandinistas in Carazo department was weak. While Diriamba was in FSLN hands, the GN held Jinotepe without any of the forces going on the offensive. About 300 FSLN fighters were organized in 10 platoons, of three squads of 10 men each. Each platoon had a .30-calibre machine gun or a MG-42, and a bazooka with 10 rockets. They also had two .50-calibre machine guns, one BZ

and two mortars. They left Diriamba by truck on 4 July. In Jinotepe, the 200 men of the GN were dispersed in 16 barracks under the orders of Rafael Lola. The FSLN plan was simple: attack relentlessly to isolate each barracks.[315]

The attack began on the morning of 5 July with Sandinista forces attacking all the barracks at the same time. They put the GN tanks out of action and prevented the troops from moving. By noon, the FSLN controlled half of the city. It took two days to take the communications building. Some barracks were taken but others surrendered, such as that commanded by Captain Espinales. Fighting continued in the city at night, the Sandinistas progressing gradually. Rafael Lola and the GN leaders took advantage of the darkness to flee Jinotepe towards Granada. On the morning of the 6th, the city fell, as did San Marcos. The regime's lines of communication from Managua towards Granada, Rivas and the south were thus cut.[316]

The capture of Jinotepe was a severe blow to the Somoza regime, preventing it from conducting a counteroffensive. In order to improve his position, Somoza had to focus his efforts mainly on the south-east and west. By taking Diriamba, he could still have neutralized the advance of the Southern Front and then concentrated his forces to attack León and Chinandega. The loss of Jinotepe made it impossible to realise this plan.[317]

On 6 July, three GN helicopters bombed Masaya while mortars and cannons in the fortress of El Coyotepe pounded Sandinista trenches. Meanwhile, in Carazo, Sandinista forces consolidated their victory, the positions at Diriamba were fortified and order restored in San Marcos. Sandinistas also recovered hundreds of thousands of ammunition rounds, plus machine guns, hand grenades, Garand, M16 and Galil rifles and dynamite. These weapons helped to strengthen the defence of the liberated area.[318]

The Central Front also received military supplies by air for its next objective, the capture of Granada. While Masaya was still under fire from the fortress of El Coyotepe, the FSLN had about 250 well-armed men in the town who could defend the area, without counting the militia forces. They then replaced the Rolando Orozco battalion squads who guarded the strategic trenches for the defence of the city, after which the FSLN had more than 1,000 fighters to achieve its next goal: Granada.

Negotiations in Puntarenas

In the first week of July, helped by Pezzullo and Ambler H. Moss, US ambassador to Panama, William Bowdler tried to find a negotiated solution to the crisis and asked the FSLN to appoint moderate elements within an enlarged JGRN. At a meeting in Palo Alto on 8 July, Tomás Borge, Carlos Nunez, Henry Ruiz, Daniel Ortega, Victor Tirado and Humberto Ortega decided to reject this proposal. On 11 July, President Rodrigo Carazo of Costa Rica, Bowdler, Humberto Ortega and Tomás Borge, as well as JGRN members Violeta Chamorro, Sergio Ramirez and Daniel Ortega, met in the port of Puntarenas. Former presidents José Figueres (Costa Rica) and Carlos Andrés Pérez (Venezuela) also joined the meeting, which rejected the idea of expanding the JGRN.

On the 12th, after a meeting with Bowdler and representatives of Costa Rica, Panama and Venezuela, the Sandinistas reached an agreement on a peace plan. It provided for the resignation of Somoza, the transfer of power to the FSLN, the dissolution of Congress, a ceasefire and immunity for the GN and Somoza supporters who had not committed any crimes. It also stipulated the formation of a 30-member State Council with representatives of religious, professional and academic organisations, and the establishment of a mixed economy combining public enterprises, private companies and cooperatives. On the military side, the Puntarenas Pact planned to create a new army bringing together GN members who had not committed crimes and Sandinista guerrillas.[319]

On 15 July, the Sandinistas adopted two measures to ensure US support for the FSLN: the formation of an 18-member cabinet in which the moderates would have the majority and a promise to invite the OAS to ensure human rights by the new government.[320] After the meeting in Puntarenas, a transition plan was worked out, but a meeting between the head of the GN and Humberto Ortega failed to achieve any concrete agreement.

By this time, dozens of towns and villages, along with entire departments, were in FSLN hands, with others about to be taken. The FSLN Directorate then decided to bring JGRN members into the country as quickly as possible. León was declared free territory on 9 July, and on the 15th Daniel Ortega arrived there by plane with Tomás Borge and Rosarío Murillo, being received by Jaime Wheelock and Dora María Téllez.

In Palo Alto, the leadership of the FSLN, in agreement with the commanders of the various fronts, insisted on the need for the total capitulation of the enemy, using the Puntarenas agreement as an assurance of salvation for the GN troops. The FSLN feared that if the war continued, it would be difficult for it to thwart a ceasefire imposed by the mediation of foreign troops, which the US wished to implement. The FSLN sought to achieve through dialogue with the new GN head the total surrender of the military, to avoid a bloodbath in Managua.[321]

Taking of Granada

The Central Front was commissioned to seize Granada, for which it had the Rolando Orozco Battalion. They also had to seize Diria and Diríomo in the early hours of 18 July in order to prevent the troops in Granada withdrawing to Rivas, and avoid blows from Rivas by attacking Nandaime. Once these objectives were achieved, they had to prepare the troops to march on Managua in convergence with the Western, Northern and Eastern Fronts. An insurgency in Granada appeared very risky to FSLN officials as the city contained many GN forces, reinforced by those fleeing the surrounding areas and also from the south.

On the morning of the 17 July, the mobile battalion of Rolando Orozco attacked Granada after reaching the outskirts of the city by truck. The eight platoons took action simultaneously at all points. The fighting lasted all day, with frontal attacks and house to house fighting.

The FSLN seized the centre of Granada, the *Palacio de Comunicaciones* and the cathedral, the steeples of the latter having been used by GN snipers. About of the 300 GN took refuge in the main barracks of La Pólvora, where they found themselves encircled on the morning of the 18th.[322] The same day, platoons attacked the garrisons of Diria and Diríomo in an effort to prevent the sending of GN reinforcements to Granada and any escape of military Somozists.[323]

The Sandinista strategy involved a guerrilla movement across Granada and along the road to Nandaime, north of Rivas, to overpower the concentrated GN forces south of Rivas. Guerrillas managed to blockade 600 soldiers in their garrison at Rivas. The attacks launched on Nandaime, and the GN's isolation in Granada, Diria and Diríomo, made impossible any links with EEBI stationed in Rivas and on the Southern Front. On 18 July, with the GN besieged in its barracks in Granada, negotiations began with their commander, Colonel Ruiz, who accepted callas for their surrender.[324]

After the fall of Jinotepe and Granada, fighting in the central region was concentrated against the fortress of El Coyotepe in Masaya. Finally, on 19 July, GN troops abandoned this position, allowing the reopening of the Pan-American Highway under Sandinista control.

The Twilight of Somozism

On the evening of 16 July, Somoza presented his resignation to the Nicaraguan Congress during an emergency session at the Intercontinental Hotel. From 11:00 p.m. that night, his aides began assembling a military convoy, commanded by Colonel Jerónimo Linarte, that was to take the former dictator and his relatives to Las Mercedes Airport. The buses were ready at 3:00 a.m. and parked at the main entrance of the Intercontinental, but the column only began moving at 4:00 a.m. Even then, Somoza didn't travel by road: a helicopter picked him up from the top of a nearby hill and flew him out to Las Mercedes.

Somoza's son, Colonel Somoza Portocarrero, insisted on continuing to fight with the EEBI troops, although his father ordered him to be at the airport by 4:00 a.m.: in a final act of rebellion, the son arrived at least 35 minutes late. Nevertheless, he was the first to be flown out on board a Convair 880, with Somoza Debayle following on a de Havilland 125-600 at 5:00 a.m, both heading into exile in the USA.[325]

After the acceptance of the resignation of Somoza, Congress appointed Francisco Urcuyo Maleafios the new head of state. President Urcuyo then amazed US officials and opposition leaders by stating

Similar to the situation in Saigon in 1975, once the Somozas left the country, the US rushed to evacuate its citizens from Nicaragua, with Lockheed C-130E Hercules transports of the US Air Force Reserve starting to land at Las Mercedes IAP on 18 July. (US DoD)

A USAFRES C-130E on the tarmac of Las Mercedes IAP, about to embark dozens of US civilians (the family in the foreground was turned back because the aircraft was already full). (US DoD)

Helicopters from the amphibious assault ship USS *Saipan* (LHA-2) were also involved in the evacuation of Americans and other foreigners from Nicaragua. (US Navy photo)

The Spanish Air Force also took part in the evacuation of expatriates from Nicaragua in July 1979. This C-130H was from the 301st Squadron of the Spanish Air Force. (via Mark Lepko)

to fight communism, hoping that by resisting it would be possible to engage Carter in a military intervention. On the night of 17 July, Somoza, from the US, urged Urcuyo and Mejia to resist, announcing the upcoming arrival of reinforcements. The latter then decided to continue the Somoza 'adventure'.[327]

The US ambassador and American diplomats left Managua in protest against Urcuyo's position. Less than 24 hours later, the latter finally resigned and gave up his powers to the JGRN before fleeing to Miami. On 18 July, from Palo Alto, Dionisio Nicho Marenco established a radio link with General Mejía. Humberto Ortega initiated discussions with him, with the participation of Archbishop Obando y Bravo. In the eyes of the FSLN, the Puntarenas agreement no longer existed because of Urcuyo's declarations and the only way out of the crisis was the GN's unconditional surrender. Ortega even threatened to storm Managua, but added that the FSLN would apply international agreements for the treatment of Somozist prisoners of war and called for an appeal from GN military leaders for all troops to lay down their arms.

General Mejía proposed a bilateral ceasefire which the FSLN, which dominated the military situation, rejected. In the early hours of 19 July, Mejía decided to resign, failing to reach a ceasefire under the terms he proposed, and gave the GN command to Colonel Fulgencio Largaespada.[328] The departure of Urcuyo and General Mejía had left the US empty-handed, without any plan to directly or indirectly influence the outcome of the crisis. The danger of their direct intervention thus became greater and seriously worried the FSLN, who wanted to avoid a bloodbath when taking Managua, which could have provided a pretext for the US to intervene.

that he intended to exercise his mandate until its statutory end in 1981.[326] The Puntarenas agreement began to collapse. Simultaneously, General Mejía, in charge of the GN, reiterated that he would continue

For this it was necessary to obtain from the GN staff a call for the surrender of its soldiers. Largaespada then received from Palo Alto the text of the unconditional surrender, which he read immediately on the GN radio circuit so that all troops that still resisted could hear him.

Sandinista victory

On 17 and 18 July, GN garrisons in León, Somoto, Ocotal, Nagarote and Boaco capitulated. During this period, guerrillas organised the ambush of a GN convoy en route to León, killing 20 soldiers. Orders to continue the fight were given to the GN by radio broadcasts from the Bunker until 18 July. In reality, the GN had ceased to be a fighting force. In the early hours of 19 July, General Mejía and members of his staff left the country by plane, abandoning the soldiers to their fate.

The Southern Front concentrated its forces, gathered its artillery and intensified its actions. Edén Pastora, moved to Cibalsa – the GN base of operations – at dawn on 18 July, with more than 2,000 men and 200 vehicles. The GN abandoned its positions in the early hours of 19 July. 'Commander Bravo' left the country, while his 1,200 soldiers fled through San Juan del Sur to get to El Salvador. On 19 July, Commander Alvaro Diroy ordered his forces to attack all GN positions at Rivas. The city fell with the help of a guerrilla column that was in La Calera at the initiative of Francisco Serrano Cuadra, who supported the column of Francisco Gutiérrez with artillery, mortars, machine guns and RPG-2s. Before noon, the Rivas barracks was taken after being burned by the GN, who fled to San Juan del Sur.[329] The war on the Southern Front ended that day with the fall of Rivas around noon. Part of the Front then moved towards Managua.

The Northern Front then seized Boaco, while the Western Front took control of the León department after hard fighting in Izapa against the EEBI. Elsewhere, Chinandega was in FSLN hands and León forces were marching on Managua. The Eastern Front, with the column of Camilo Chamorro, formed in April 1979 under the command of Luis Carrión, carried out offensive actions and seized Rama, Presillas, Santo Tomás and Juigalpa. Matagalpa and Estelí were controlled by the Northern Front, whose troops met those advancing from Chontales in San Benito; together, on 19 July, they seized Las Mercedes airport without meeting much resistance. From the west, Sandinista forces were also approaching Managua.[330]

The march on the capital was organised the same day, with the Northern and Western Fronts penetrating into the city. Sandinista forces now controlled the entire country, including Managua's three strategic communication routes: the North Highway, the Western Highway and the South Highway. In the early afternoon, Central Front forces, including the Rolando Orozco battalion, left Masaya for Managua. The insurgents entered the capital cautiously because many GN soldiers had changed into civilian clothes while attempting to disappear. The Rolando Orozco battalion seized the EEBI barracks, its fighters equipping themselves with uniforms, boots and berets. For the rest of the day, the FSLN was busy deploying its units to protect vital installations and prevent looting.

Troops of the Northern Front were the first to arrive at the Bunker, with the column Óscar Turcios and Facundo Picado, plus part of the column Filemón Rivera. They seized the complex without difficulty, since only a few gardeners and cooks remained.[331]

The Sandinista National Directorate met on 20 July at Piedrecitas, then marched with guerrillas from all Fronts and their leaders towards Managua. The Southern Front was the last to reach the capital on the morning of 20 July, just in time to participate in the victory celebration alongside the JGRN and people gathered in Republic Square, later renamed the Plaza de la Revolucion.[332]

On 24 July, Washington officially recognized the new government. A month later, the JGRN formed the Sandinista People's Army, led by Humberto Ortega. Its headquarters was established in the Somoza Bunker, renamed Chipote in memory of an operation led by Sandino; 45 years after his assassination, he was finally avenged.

The date 19 July 1979 marked a turning point in the history of Nicaragua and the FSLN. Not only had a powerful dictatorship that reigned over the country for nearly 40 years, with the support of the

Sandinistas entering Managua atop a captured Staghound armoured car to a tumultuous welcome by the local population. (Tom Cooper Collection)

Leaders of the Sandinista National Direction presenting themselves as the new government of Nicaragua on 20 July 1979. (via Mark Lepko)

US, ended, but the long and patient fight started by the Sandinistas in the early 1960s finally came to fruition. After a fight of nearly 20 years, David ended up defeating Goliath. For many years, the FSLN had only been a minor force, with no political or military weight, regularly on the brink of extinction.

Various factors explained the final Sandinista victory. The main one was the rise in the general dissatisfaction of the population, a dissatisfaction that affected all classes of society. The UDEL's formation in 1974 was a first warning that the dictatorship refused to hear. This bourgeois opposition was quickly caught between an increasingly repressive dictatorship and a more bellicose and increasingly independent popular movement. Until the end of 1978, supported by the Catholic Church and US, it tried to find a negotiated way out of the crisis, without the FSLN. It was Somoza's intransigence that pushed the opposition to join the Sandinistas, whose strength continued to grow. But this union of the bourgeois opposition and the Sandinistas was still not enough to overthrow Somoza. The dictator only definitively lost the game when Washington finally ended its support for him.[333]

While political and diplomatic factors are essential to understanding the fall of Somoza, the dominant issue was the military struggle between the FSLN and the dictatorship. Given the political and social situation of Nicaragua, the Sandinistas adopted an appropriate strategy. Although the FSLN was part of a rural guerrilla tradition, initiated by Sandino himself and relying on the Maoist, Guevarist and Vietnamese models, it rediscovered, little by little, the insurrectional strategy defined by the Comintern in the early 1920s. According to this concept, in a moment characterised by the weakening of power on one side and a growing popular unrest on the other, it was the duty of the revolutionaries to launch an insurrection. The latter had to be carefully prepared by a structured military apparatus to lead an insurgent population to first strike the centres of military and political power in the cities.

This insurrectional strategy was dominant in the 1920s and 1930s in the communist world before its failures in Europe, and also in Brazil in 1935, before the Chinese example eclipsed it. It was rediscovered in Nicaragua by the Tercerists, and Joaquin Cuadra explained that after the September 1978 offensive the FSLN's main executives began to study the writings of Lenin on the urban insurrection, along with *The Armed Insurrection* by Neuberg and *Theory of Insurrection* by Emilio Lussu.[334]

In accordance with this strategy, the FSLN had a military apparatus with guerrilla columns and Tactical Combat Units in the cities, while the insurrection of Monimbo in February 1978 showed that popular anger had reached a point of incandescence. The conditions of an insurrectional strategy were then met. A first attempt took place in October 1978, and a final one that would be victorious in the spring of 1979. As Humberto Ortega remarked, the Sandinistas had over time managed to master the art of armed insurrection, which was "a special type of political struggle," and maintain a constant and uninterrupted offensive.[335]

But the FSLN also knew how to adapt this strategy to the Nicaragua situation. By combining an urban and rural guerrilla insurgency, it managed to diminish the flaws of each. The insurgency made it possible to strike at the heart of the cities, where the majority of the population and the centres of power were, while the rural guerrillas made possible the development of an organised military force. The combination of these two forms of the revolutionary war even allowed the Sandinistas success in conventional warfare on the Southern Front. For this, it had overcome one of the weaknesses of the insurgency: the lack of weapons necessary to confront a modern military. Without weapons, the FSLN could win a few battles – but not a war.

The arms received from abroad - from Cuba, Costa Rica or Panama - played a decisive role in hastening the victory and decided, in certain respects, the fate of battles which, without weapons, would have been lost. They made it possible to form formidable units like the columns of Rolando Orozco and Óscar Pérez Cassar. Defeats would have certainly cooled the insurgency spirit in the population: while the victory of the FSLN depended heavily on the will of the people to fight, possession of 'technology' – rocket-propelled grenades, explosives and advanced firearms – played a strategic role. Furthermore, the general strike, the urban insurrection and the military offensive mutually supported each other to lead to Somoza's defeat. The strike paralysed the country, depriving the dictatorship of supplies. The insurrection dispersed GN forces throughout the territory while the Fronts relentlessly exhausted the GN's potential. Abandoned by the international community, and particularly by Washington, Somoza could no longer govern and had to flee.

Somoza's defeat was also the result of inherent weaknesses in the GN. Despite modern weaponry, this force was more a family than professional army. It only took the announcement of Somoza's departure for it to collapse completely, including the elite EEBI troops. If diverse attempts to find an alternative to Somoza all failed, then to a large degree this was because the GN was not a professional army that in times of crisis was able to place its survival as an institution above its fidelity to its boss. It was born with the Somoza dynasty, grew up in its image to become a pillar of the rule of the regime, but had no autonomy apart from the dictator, whose fall mechanically led to its disappearance.

Somoza's greatest strategic error was the ruthless repression he exerted, particularly after the 1978 uprising, when the cities were bombed, and the population subjected to summary executions without any motive, especially the young. From that moment, for thousands of Nicaraguans, the fight against Somoza was no longer a political choice but a means of defending one's life.[336] The dictatorship and the GN were then irretrievably isolated.

On 20 July 1979, it appeared that an entirely new, bright future lay ahead for Nicaragua. Most of the economy was severely disrupted, if not ruined; some cities, like Estelí, were completely destroyed; and according to various estimates, up to 75,000 people died in the last two years of Somoza's rule.[337] As tragic as it was, this chapter was over, and the new government and the people of Nicaragua were looking forward to rebuild their country.

Unknown to the Sandinistas and the Nicaraguans in general was that factors well outside their powers were about to conspire against them: only five months before the fall of the Somozas, the USA lost its major ally in the Middle East, the Shah of Iran; five months later, the Soviets invaded Afghanistan. For a while at least, it appeared as if Moscow might establish itself in a dominant position in the Middle East and Central America. The time was thus ripe for the US to strike back and the Cold War to heat up in a way not seen since 1962 and the Cuban Missile Crisis.

Selected Bibliography

Alegria, Claribel, and Flakoll, D.J., *Nicaragua: la revolucion Sandinista una cronica politica 1855-1979* (Era, 1982).

Anderson, Michael John, *Puppet Wars: The Nicaraguan Revolution in a Cold War Context* (Western Oregon University, 2003).

Aravena, Francisco, 'La Unión Soviética y Centroamérica', *Foro Internacional*, vol.28, no.4 (April-June 1988).

Avilés Farré, Juan, 'Dos guerras en Nicaragua, 1978-1988', *Espacio, Tiempo y Forma*, t.4 (1991).

Bacchetta, Victor L., 'El desmoronamiento político de un ejercito. La Gardia Nacional Somocista', *Nueva Sociedad*, no.81 (January-February 1986).

Barbosa Miranda, Francisco, *Síntesis de la historia militar de Nicaragua* (Centro de Historia militar-ejercito de Nicaragua, 2007).

Bataillon, Gilles, *Genèse des guerres internes en Amérique centrale (1960-1983)* (Les Belles Lettres, 2003).

Bataillon, Gilles, 'De Sandino aux Contras. Formes et pratique de la guerre au Nicaragua', *Annales HSS*, no.3, (May-June 2005).

Booth, John A., *The End and the Beginning: The Nicaraguan Revolution* (Westview Press, 1982).

Borge Martínez, Tomás, *La paciente imapaciencia* (Casas de la Américas, 1989).

Bulmer-Thomas, Victor, 'Nicaragua desde 1930', in Bethell, Leslie (ed.), *Historia de America latina, 14. America Central desde 1930* (Critica, 2001).

Cabezas, Omar, *La montaña es algo más que una immensa estepa verde* (Nueva Nicaragua, 1982).

Clark, Alexander Bjorn, *Carter confronts Somoza: When Lofty Ideals Collide with Cold War Realities* (University of Montana, 2013).

Diederich, Bernard, *Somoza and the Legacy of U.S. Involvement in Central America* (E.P. Dutton, 1981).

Fernández Hellmund, Paula, 'La fractura del movimiento revolucionarío: tendencias dentro del Frente Sandinista de Liberación Nacional (1972-1979)', *Cuaderno de Martes*, no.4 (July 2013).

Fernández Hellmund, Paula, 'Quiten la manos de Nicaragua! Solidaridad argentina con la revolution Sandinista (1979-1990)', *Si Somos Americanos. Revista de Estudios Transfonterizos*, vol.13, no.2 (July-December 2013).

Ferrero Blanco, María-Dolores, 'Violencia y represión en el ocaso de los Somoza: la condiciones carcelarias de los presos politicos', *Historia Crítica*, no.39 (September-December 2009).

Ferrero Blanco, María-Dolores, 'Las relaciones de los Somoza de Nicaragua con EE.UU. (1936-1979)', *Hispania Nova*, no.10 (2012).

Ferrero Blanco, María-Dolores, *La Nicaragua de los Somoza: 1936-1979* (Universidad de Huelva, 2012).

García Marquez, Gabriel, *El Asalto* (Editorial Nueva Nicaragua, 1982).

Gilbert, Dennis, *Sandinistas: The Party and the Revolution* (Basil Blackwell, 1988).

Harnecker, Marta, *Pueblos en armas* (Nueva Nicaragua, 1985).

Hassan, Moisés, *La malédiction du Güegüense. Anatomie de la révolution sandiniste* (Les Belles Lettres, 2016).

Hernandez, Myrna, *From base organization to mass mobilization in Nicaragua: the case of Estelí* (Durham University, 1982).

Hernández Sancho, Plutarco, *El FSLN por dentro. Relatos de un combatiente* (Trejos Hermanos, 1982).

Hoffman, Bruce, *The PLO and Israel in Central America: The Geopolitical Dimension* (Rand Corporation, 1988).

Ignatiev, Oleg, and Borovik, Genrykh, *The Agony of Dictatorship: Nicaraguan Chronicle* (Progress Publishers, 1980).

Jaramillo, Jorge F., *Successful Insurgent Revolutions in Latin America: Analysis of the Cuban and Nicaraguan Revolutions* (Naval Postgraduate School, Monterey, 2015).

Kagan, Robert, *A Twilight Struggle: American Power and Nicaragua, 1977-1990* (The Free Press, 1996).

Keen, Benjamin, and Haynes, Keith, *A History of Latin America* (Houghton Mifflin Company, 2000).

Kinzer, Stephen, *Blood and Brothers. Life and War in Nicaragua* (Putnam, 1991).

Le Blanc, Jörg Heinrich Christopher, *Political Violence in Latin America. A Cross-Case Comparison of the Urban Insurgency Campaigns of Montoneros, M-19, and FSLN in a Historical Perspective* (Amsterdam University, 2012).

Martí i Puig, Salvador, *La Révolución enredada, Nicaragua, 1977-1996* (Los Libros de la Catarata, 1997).

Martí i Puig, Salvador, *La izquiedra revoluctionaria en Centroamérica: El FSLN desde su fundación a la insurrección popular* (Universitat Autònoma de Barcelona, 2002).

Millen, Raymond, *The political context behind successful revolutionary movements, three case studies: Vietnam (1955-63), Algeria (1945-62), Nicaragua 1967-79)* (US Army War College, 2008).

Millet, Richard, *Guardians of the Dynasty: A History of the US Created Guardia Nacional de Nicaragua and the Somoza Family* (Orbis Books, 1977).

Monroy-García, Juan José, *Tendencias ideológico-políticas des Frente Sandinista de libéracion nacional, 1975-1990* (Universitad Autónoma del Estado de México, 1997).

Morley, Morris H., *Washington, Somoza, and the Sandinistas* (Cambridge University Press, 1994).

Nuñez Téllez, Carlos, *Un pueblo en armas* (Vanguardia, 1986).

Ortega, Humberto, *La epopeya de la insurrección* (Lea Grupo Editorial, 2004).

Pérez, Cristián, 'Compañeros, A las armas: combatientes chilenos en Centroamérica (1979-1989)', *Estudios Públicos*, 129 (summer 2013).

Pisani, Francis, *Muchachos. Nicaragua, journal d'un témoin de la révolution sandiniste* (Encre, 1980).

Ramirez, Sergio, *La marca del zorro, hazanas del commandante Francisco Rivera Quintero* (Editorial Nueva Nicaragua, 1989).

Richmond, John D., *The Armed Citizen Pillar of Democracy* (Air Command and Staff College, Air University, 2010).

Schroeder, Michael J., *The Sandino Rebellion* (www.sandinorebellion. com).

Seligson, Mitchell A., and Carroll III, William J., 'The Costa Rican Role in the Sandinista Victory', *in* Walker, Thomas W. (ed.), *Nicaragua in Revolution* (Prager, 1982).

Sierakowski, Robert James, *In the Footsteps of Sandino: Geographies of Revolution and Political Violence in Northern Nicaragua, 1956-1979* (PhD Dissertation, University of California, 2012).

Somoza Debayle, Anastasio, and Cox, Jack, *Nicaragua Betrayed* (Western Islands, 1980).

Tinelli, Giorgio, *La cultura politica des sandinismo: nacimiento, desarollo y realineamiento de une anomalia politica centroamericano* (Universidad Complutense Madrid, 2015).

Vayssière, Pierre, *Auguste Cesar Sandino ou l'envers d'un mythe* (Presses du CNRS, 1988).

Walker, Thomas W., *Nicaragua, the land of Sandino* (Westview Press, 1979).

Walker, Thomas W. (ed.), *Nicaragua in Revolution* (Praeger, 1985).

Walker, Thomas W., *Nicaragua, Living in the Shadow of the Eagle* (Westview Press, 2003).

Weathers, Bynum E, *Guerrilla Warfare in Nicaragua* (Air University Research Study, 1983).

Wilson, Andrew W., *Conflict beyond Borders: The International Dimensions of Nicaragua's Violent Twentieth Century, 1909-1990* (University of Nebraska, 2016).

Zimmerman, Matilde, *Sandinista: Carlos Fonseca and the Nicaraguan Revolution* (Duke University Press, 2003).

Further information used in this book was obtained from diverse websites and online archives, such as those of the cia. org, nsa.org, the Library of Congress Country Studies, gaf.mil.gh, memoriasdelaluchaSandinista.org and nicaraocalli.wordpress.com.

Notes

1. The Communist International, or Comintern, was founded in Moscow by Lenin in 1919 and advocated world communism. It was dissolved in 1943.
2. Lenin, Vladimir Ilich Ulyanov, *Marxism and Insurrection, Collected Works* (Moscow: Progress Publishers, 1972), Vol. 26, pp.22-27.
3. Bataillon, Gilles, *Genèse des guerres internes en Amérique centrale (1960-1983)* (Paris: Les Belles Lettres, 2003), pp.36-39.
4. Ruigómez, Manuel Hernandez, *La Nicaragua sandinista y las elecciones de febrero 1990: transición a la democracia o alternancia democrática* (Madrid: Universidade Complutense de Madrid, 2011), p.51.
5. Walker, Thomas W., *Nicaragua, Living in the Shadow of the Eagle* (Colorado: Westview Press, 2003), p.10.
6. Ruigómez, Manuel Hernandez, pp.54-55.
7. *Ibidem*, p.57.
8. Richmond, John D., *The Armed Citizen Pillar of Democracy* (Montgomery, Alabama: Air Command and Staff College, Air University, 2010), p.4.
9. Ruigómez, Manuel Hernandez p.58.
10. Seligson, Mitchell A., and Carroll III, William J., 'The Costa Rican Role in the Sandinista Victory', in Walker, Thomas W. (ed.), *Nicaragua in Revolution* (New York, Praeger, 1982), p.332.
11. Wilson, Andrew W., *Conflict beyond Borders: The International Dimensions of Nicaragua's Violent Twentieth-Century, 1909-1990* (Lincoln, USA: University of Nebraska, 2016), pp.22-23.
12. Ruigómez, Manuel Hernandez, p.61.
13. *Ibidem*, pp.66-67.
14. Bulmer-Thomas, Victor, 'Nicaragua desde 1930', in Bethell, Leslie (ed.), *Historia de America latina, 14. America Central desde 1930* (Barcelona: Critica, 2001), p.145.
15. Ruigómez, Manuel Hernandez, p.70.
16. Wilson, Andrew W., pp.24-5.
17. Ruigómez, Manuel Hernandez, p.73.
18. *Ibidem*, pp.71-72.
19. Bataillon, Gilles, 'De Sandino aux Contras. Formes et pratique de la guerre au Nicaragua', in *Annales HSS*, No.3, May-June 2005, p.657.
20. Bulmer-Thomas, Victor, p.147.
21. Keen, Benjamin, and Haynes, Keith, *A History of Latin America* (Boston: Houghton Mifflin Company, 2000), p.470.
22. Pisani, Francis, *Muchachos. Nicaragua, journal d'un témoin de la révolution Sandiniste* (Paris: Encre, 1980), p.24.
23. Richmond, John D., p.9.
24. Bulmer-Thomas, Victor, p.151.
25. APRA was founded in Mexico City in 1924. It was a transnational nationalist and revolutionary Latin American organization that wanted to fight against North American imperialism and for the nationalization of lands and industries. Iglesias, Daniel, 'L'Alliance populaire révolutionnaire américaine (APRA) comme dynamique transnationale. Du réseau à la fabrication d'un discours nationaliste', in *Cahiers des Amériques latines*, 66, 2011, pp.111-29.
26. Bulmer-Thomas, Victor, p.154.
27. Wilson, Andrew W., p.30.
28. Aravena, Francisco Rojas, 'La Unión Soviética y Centroamérica', in *Foro Internacional*, vol.28, no.4, April-June 1988, p.820.
29. Bulmer-Thomas, Victor, p.156.
30. Sierakowski, Robert James, *In the Footsteps of Sandino: Geographies of Revolution and Political Violence in Northern Nicaragua, 1956-1979* (PhD dissertation, University of California, 2012), pp.33-34.
31. It was not until 1939 that the GN definitively put out of action the handful of Sandinista fighters who continued the fight in various guerrilla groups under the command of Pedro Altamirano.
32. Bulmer-Thomas, Victor, p.156.
33. Monroy-García, Juan José, *Tendencias ideológico-políticas des Frente Sandinista de libéracion nacional, 1975-1990* (Toluca: Universidad Autónoma del Estado de México, 2015), p.33.
34. *Ibidem*, p.35.
35. Bulmer-Thomas, Victor, p.160.
36. *Ibidem*, p.160.
37. Ferrero Blanco, María-Dolores, 'Las relaciones de los Somoza de Nicaragua con EE.UU. (1936-1979)', in *Hispania Nova*, no.10, 2012, p.59.
38. Bulmer-Thomas, Victor, p.161.
39. *Ibidem*, p.162.
40. Monroy-García, Juan José, p.36.
41. Ferrero Blanco, María-Dolores, 'Las relaciones de los Somoza de Nicaragua con EE.UU. (1936-1979)', pp.62-64.
42. Le PSN, fondée en 1944, operated as the official Communist Party in Nicaragua.
43. Tinelli, Giorgio, *La cultura politica des sandinismo: nacimiento, desarollo y realineamiento de une anomalia politica centroamericano* (doctoral thesis, Universidas Complutense de Madrid, 2016), p.116.
44. Farré, Juan Avilés, 'Dos guerras en Nicaragua, 1978-1988',in *Espacio, Tiempo y Forma*, vol.4, 1991, p.294.
45. Tinelli, Giorgio, p.124.
46. Ruigómez, Manuel Hernandez, p.96.
47. Bulmer-Thomas, Victor, p.167.
48. Bacchetta, Víctor L., 'El desmoronamiento político de un ejercito. La Gardia Nacional Somocista', in *Nueva Sociedad*, no.81, January-February 1986, p.20.
49. Wilson, Andrew W., p.109.
50. Monroy-García, Juan José, p.38.
51. Bulmer-Thomas, Victor, p.169.

52 *Ibidem*, p.169.

53 Monroy-García, Juan José, p.41.

54 Bulmer-Thomas, Victor, p.169.

55 Pisani, Francis, *Muchachos. Nicaragua, journal d'un témoin de la révolution Sandinistae* (Paris: Encre, 1980), p.25.

56 Sierakowski, Robert James, p.96.

57 Wilson, Andrew W., pp.142-47.

58 Barbosa Miranda, Francisco, *Síntesis de la historia militar de Nicaragua* (Managua: Centro de Historia militar-ejercito de Nicaragua, 2007), pp.45-50.

59 On 23 July 1959, students from León demonstrated for the liberation of guerrillas captured in El Chaparral. The GN violently dispersed the demonstrators, causing the death of four students while about 70 were wounded.

60 Ruigómez, Manuel Hernandez, p.102.

61 Le Blanc, Jörg Heinrich Christopher, *Political Violence in Latin America. A Cross-Case Comparison of the Urban Insurgency Campaigns of Montoneros, M-19, and FSLN in a Historical Perspective* (Amsterdam: Amsterdam University, 1979), p.189.

62 Sierakowski, Robert James, pp.98-99.

63 Monroy-García, Juan José, p.44.

64 The 'foco' theory was elaborated by Che Guevara and exposed by Régis Debray in his book *Revolution in the Revolution*. According to Guevara, the guerrilla was an armed vanguard of the people for military actions to seize power. The insurgent 'foco' began as a small guerrilla group that settled on a territory that it had chosen, knowing its environment and establishing links with the population. With time, the guerrillas had to grow and consolidate while developing political work among the population before becoming a popular army.

65 Wilson, Andrew W., pp.170-71.

66 Monroy-García, Juan José, p.45.

67 Weathers, Bynum E., *Guerrilla Warfare in Nicaragua* (Montgomery, Alabama: Air University Research Study, 1983), p.4.

68 Anderson, Michael John, *Puppet Wars: The Nicaraguan Revolution in a Cold War Context* (Monmouth, Oregon: Western Oregon University, 2003), p.14.

69 Weathers, Bynum E., p.5.

70 Jaramillo, Jorge F., *Successful Insurgent Revolutions in Latin America: Analysis of the Cuban and Nicaraguan Revolutions* (Monterey: Naval Postgraduate School, 2015), p.59.

71 Monroy-García, Juan José, p.55.

72 Diederich, Bernard, *Somoza and the Legacy of U.S. Involvement in Central America* (Boston: E.P. Dutton, 1981), p.85.

73 Selim Shible initiated armed robbery against banks to finance the FSLN. He died age just 23.

74 Monroy-García, Juan José, pp.46-47.

75 *Ibidem*, pp.62-63.

76 Sierakowski, Robert James, p.97.

77 Jaramillo, Jorge F., p.61.

78 Monroy-García, Juan José, p.67.

79 *Ibidem*, pp.49-50.

80 Bataillon, Gilles, p.130.

81 Barbosa Miranda, Francisco, p.36.

82 Bacchetta, Víctor L., p.23.

83 Gambone, Michael D., *Eisenhower, Somoza and the Cold War in Nicaragua, 1953-1961* (Praeger, 1997), p.112.

84 Bacchetta, Víctor L., pp.24-25.

85 Ferrero Blanco, María-Dolores, *La Nicaragua de los Somoza: 1936-1979* (Universidad de Huelva, 2012), p.40.

86 *Ibidem*, p.118.

87 Barbosa Miranda, Francisco, p.40.

88 Bacchetta, Víctor L., p.31.

89 https://archive.org/details/CIA-RDP80T00942A001100130001-8.

90 Pisani, Francis, p.36.

91 Wilson, Andrew W., p.150.

92 Hagedorn, Dan & Hellström, Leif, p.92.

93 Hagedorn, Dan & Hellström, Leif, pp.93-94.

94 *Ibidem*, p.95.

95 Jaramillo, Jorge F., p. 98.

96 Sierakowski, Robert James, p. 71.

97 *Ibidem*, pp.67-68.

98 Bacchetta, Víctor L., p.27.

99 Ferrero Blanco, María-Dolores, *La Nicaragua de los Somoza*, p.369.

100 Sierakowski, Robert James, pp.207-09.

101 Le Blanc, Jörg Heinrich Christopher, p.214.

102 Sierakowski, Robert James, pp.194-95.

103 Ferrero Blanco, María-Dolores, *La Nicaragua de los Somoza*, p.363.

104 Bacchetta, Víctor L., p.32.

105 Diederich, Bernard, p.186.

106 Ferrero Blanco, María-Dolores, *La Nicaragua de los Somoza*, p.364.

107 https://www.laprensa.com.ni/2015/07/19/suplemento/la-prensa-domingo/1868933-final-la-guardia-nacional-nicaragua.

108 Sierakowski, Robert James, p.188.

109 Wilson, Andrew W., p.134.

110 Ferrero Blanco, María-Dolores, 'Las relaciones de los Somoza de Nicaragua con EE.UU', p.82.

111 Wilson, Andrew W., p.53.

112 *Ibidem*, p. 153-56.

113 *Ibidem*, p.233.

114 *Ibidem*, p.243.

115 Puig, Salvador Martí i, *La Révolución enredada, Nicaragua, 1977-1996* (Los Libros de la Catarata, 1997), p.24.

116 Monroy-García, Juan José, pp.56-58.

117 Ruiz, Henry, 'El faro que alumbró a los combatientes', in Baltodano, Monica,, *Memoria de la lucha Sandinista*, https://memoriasdelaluchaSandinista.org/view_stories.php?id=29.

118 It was designed on the model of the Ho Chi Minh Trail; Sierakowski, Robert James, pp.153-54.

119 Ruiz, Henry, 'El faro que alumbró a los combatientes', in Baltodano, Monica,, https://memoriasdelaluchaSandinista.org/view_stories.php?id=29.

120 Le Blanc, Jörg Heinrich Christopher, p.197.

121 Harnecker, Marta, *Pueblos en armas* (Managua: Nueva Nicaragua, 1985), p.61.

122 *Ibidem*, p.101.

123 Dominguez, Guillermo Cortés, *De León al Bunker* (Edidarte, 2003), p.391.

124 Harnecker, Marta, p.64.

125 *Ibidem*, p.65.

126 Le Blanc, Jörg Heinrich Christopher, p.201.

127 https://www.cia.gov/library/readingroom/document/cia-rdp83b01027r000200030003-0

128 https://www.laprensa.com.ni/2015/07/19/suplemento/la-prensa-domingo/1868933-final-la-guardia-nacional-nicaragua.

129 Wilson, Andrew W., p.173.

130 *Ibidem*, pp.177-78.

131 Hoffman, Bruce, *The PLO and Israel in Central America: The Geopolitical Dimension* (Santa Monica: Rand Corporation, 1988), p.4.

132 During this period, the FSLN applied methods promoted by Palestinians, such as the 23 December 1969 raid on a Costa Rican prison where Fonseca was imprisoned or the hijacking of a Costa Rican plane in October 1970.

133 Patricio Argüello was in the FPLP commando who tried to hijack an El Al plane between Amsterdam and New York on 6 September 1970. Faced with the resistance of Israeli security agents, the operation failed and Argüello was killed. He became a martyr for the Palestinian cause and the Sandinistas.

134 Valenta, Jiri, 'The USSR, Cuba and the Crisis in Central America', *Orbis 25*, no.3, 1981, p.734.

135 Hassan, Moisés,, *La malédiction du Güegüense. Anatomie de la révolution Sandinistae* (Paris: Les Belles Lettres, 2016), p.207.

136 Castro Ruz, Fidel, *La paz en Colombia* (Havana: Editora Politica, 2009), p.129.

137 Hassan, Moisés,, p.217.

138 Valenta, Jiri, p.735.

139 José Figueres was one of Costa Rica's most respected and influential personalities. He was the founder of the social-democratic National Liberation Party, which won the presidential elections in 1974. Figueres had long been a fierce opponent of the Somozas.

140 Bataillon, Gilles, p.172.

141 President of Venezuela since 1974, Carlos Andrés Pérez, a former trade unionist and opponent of the dictatorship, befriended Pedro Chamorro in Costa Rica.

142 Fernandez Hellmund, Paula, Quiten la manos de Nicaragua! Solidaridad argentina con la revolution Sandinista (1979-1990)', in *Si Somos Americanos. Revista de Estudios Transfonterizos*, vol.13, no.2, July-December 2013, p.36.

143 Orero, Eudald Cortina, 'Internacionalismo y Revolución Sandinista: proyecciones militantes y reformulaciones orgánicas en la izquierda revolucionaria argentina', in *Estudios Interdisciplinarios de América Latina y el Caribe*, vol.28, no.2, 2017, pp.80-103.

144 Pérez, Cristián, Compañeros, 'A las armas: combatientes chilenos en Centroamérica (1979-1989)', in *Estudios Públicos*, no.129, summer 2013, pp.141-64.

145 Castro, Fidel, pp.128-29.

146 Pisani, Francis, p.159.

147 Modesto Rojas, En qué voy ? Robate un avión', in Monica Baltodan, https://memoriasdelaluchaSandinista.org/view_stories.php?id=75.

148 Pisani, Francis, p.162.

149 Hugo Torres, 'Hoy seremos héros o mártiras', in Baltodano, Monica,, https://memoriasdelaluchaSandinista.org/view_stories.php?id=27.

150 Hassan, Moisés,, p.169.

151 Weathers, Bynum E., pp.11-13.

152 Wilson, Andrew W., p.205.

153 Weathers, Bynum E., 1983, p.14.

154 *Ibidem*, p.14.

155 Jaramillo, Jorge F., p.62.

156 Weathers, Bynum E., p.15.

157 Hassan, Moisés,, p.181.

158 Ferrero Blanco, María-Dolores, *La Nicaragua de los Somoza*, p.362.

159 *Ibidem*, p.368.

160 Weathers, Bynum E., p.15.

161 Pisani, Francis, *Muchachos*, p.73.

162 Monroy-García, Juan José, pp.58-60.

163 An FSLN member since 1969, Wheelock fled Nicaragua in 1970 to study in Allende, Chile, then in East Germany, before returning to Nicaragua in 1974.

164 Fernández Hellmund, Paula, 'La fractura del movimiento revolucionarío: tendencias dentro el Frente Sandinista de Liberación Nacional (1972-1979)', in *Cuaderno de Martes*, no.4, July 2013, p.151.

165 Monroy-García, Juan José, pp.103-04.

166 Fernández Hellmund, Paula, p.175.

167 Zimmerman, Matilde, *Sandinista: Carlos Fonseca and the Nicaraguan Revolution* (Durham, North Carolina: Duke University Press, 2003), p.192.

168 Wilson, Andrew W., pp.199-203.

169 Bataillon, Gilles, p.129.

170 Bulmer-Thomas, Victor, p.172.

171 As part of this policy, Carter signed the Treaty of Tlatelolco, which made Latin America a zone without nuclear weapons, and in September 1977 an agreement with Panama that provided for the departure of US troops from that country and the transfer of control of the Panama Canal in 2000.

172 Bataillon, Gilles, p.158.

173 Harnecker, Marta, p.20.

174 Cabezas, Omar, *La montaña es algo más que una immensa estepa verde* (Nueva Nicaragua, 1982).

175 Hugo Torres, 'La epoca de la vacas flacas en la lucha guerrillera', in Baltodano, Monica,, https://memoriasdelaluchaSandinista.org/view_stories.php?id=31.

176 *Ibidem*.

177 Pisani, Francis, pp.111-12.

178 Harnecker, Marta, p.21.

179 Pisani, Francis, *Muchachos*, p.113.

180 Baltodano, Monica 'La Segovias de Sandino. Conspiración, represión y luchas', in Baltodano, Monica,, https://memoriasdelaluchaSandinista.org/view_stories.php?id=38.

181 Ortega, Humberto, *La epopeya de la insurrección* (Lea Grupo Editorial, 2004), p.318.

182 Monroy-García, Juan José, p.119.

183 Later, part of this column settled as a guerrilla group in Macuelizo, acting specifically towards Ocotal. The rest of the fighters were sent to different places to organize the 1978 uprising.

184 Pisani, Francis, Muchachos, p.115.

185 Valdivia, José, 'Qué revolución ni qué nada, lo que queriamos era botar à Somoza !', in Baltodano, Monica,, https://memoriasdelaluchaSandinista.org/view_stories.php?id=69

186 Pisani, Francis, *Muchachos*, p.63.

187 Alfredo Sánchez, Patricia Brenes, Pedro Rivas Guatemala and Miguel Ángel Herrera, 'Un Largo y dolorosa día', in Baltodano, Monica,, https://memoriasdelaluchaSandinista.org/view_stories.php?id=71.

188 Seligson, Mitchell A., and Carroll III, William J., 'The Costa Rican Role in the Sandinista Victory', in Walker, Thomas W., (ed), *Nicaragua in Révolution* (New York: Praeger, 1982), p.333.

189 Harnecker, Marta, p.31.

190 *Ibidem*, p.54.

191 Monroy-García, Juan José, pp.114-15.

192 Clark, Alexander Bjorn, *Carter confronts Somoza: When Lofty Ideals Collide with Cold War Realities* (University of Montana, 2013), p.12.

193 Monroy-García, Juan José, pp.96-97.

194 While Somoza always claimed his innocence in the assassination of Chamorro, it seems that the murder was organized by some of his relatives, including his son, Enríquez, Octavio; 'El complot para asesinar PJCh', *La Prensa*, 10 January 2016.

195 Bataillon, Gilles, p.163.

196 Weathers, Bynum E., p.20.

197 *Ibidem*, p.21.

198 *Ibidem*, p.21.

199 Harnecker, Marta, p.60.

200 *Ibidem*, p. 8.

201 Sierakowski, Robert James, pp.248-50.

202 Harnecker, Marta, p.33.

203 Bataillon, Gilles, p.197.

204 Weathers, Bynum E., p.25.

205 Bataillon, Gilles, p.167.

206 Michael Echannis, a US citizen and veteran of the Vietnam War, was recruited as an EEBI instructor by Anastasio Somoza Portocarrero. The latter met him during his studies at the School of Psychological Warfare and Special War in Fort Bragg in North Carolina. Echannis and Chuck Charles Sander, another veteran of Vietnam, were experts in guerrilla warfare. In July 1977, they arrived in Nicaragua as special instructors of anti-guerrilla commandos.

207 Bataillon, Gilles, pp.170-71.

208 Weathers, Bynum E., pp.27-29.

209 Bataillon, Gilles, pp.176-77.

210 Weathers, Bynum E., p.30.

211 Harnecker, Marta, p.62.

212 *Ibidem*, p. 3.

213 Ulises Tapia died during the insurrection.

214 Elías Noguera Julio Ramos, 'Estelí: Indomable guerrillera', in Baltodano, Monica,, https://memoriasdelaluchaSandinista.org/view_stories.php?id=40.

215 Sierakowski, Robert James, p.260.

216 Weathers, Bynum E., p.31.

217 The population nicknamed FAN jets '*mariposas de la muerte*' (butterflies of death); Sierakowski, Robert James p.261.

218 Pisani, Francis, *Muchachos*, p.37.

219 Sierakowski, Robert James, p.267.

220 Weathers, Bynum E., p.32.

221 Pisani, Francis, *Muchachos*, p.38.

222 Monroy-García, Juan José, p.129.

223 Clark, Alexander Bjorn, p.14.

224 Weathers, Bynum E., p.33.

225 Monroy-García, Juan José, p.43.

226 Weathers, Bynum E., p.34.

227 Le Blanc, Jörg Heinrich Christopher, pp.213-14.

228 Elías Noguera Julio Ramos, 'Estelí: Indomable guerrillera', in Baltodano, Monica,, https://memoriasdelaluchaSandinista.org/view_stories.php?id=40.

229 Weathers, Bynum E., p.37.

230 *Ibidem*, p.39.

231 Valdivia, José, 'Qué revolución ni qué nada, lo que queriamos era botar à Somoza !', in Baltodano, Monica,, https://memoriasdelaluchaSandinista.org/view_stories.php?id=69.

232 On 22 November 1978, the GN killed two civilian guards in Costa Rica and captured two more.

233 Sergio Lira and José Miguel Torres, 'La masacre de El Calvario', in Baltodano, Monica,, https://memoriasdelaluchaSandinista.org/view_stories.php?id=57.

234 Weathers, Bynum E., p.42.

235 Harnecker, Marta, p.69.

236 Bataillon, Gilles, p.185.

237 Pisani, Francis, *Muchachos*, pp.299-300.

238 Fernández Hellmund, Paula, p.179.

239 Puig, Salvador Martí i, p.40.

240 Pisani, Francis, *Muchachos*, p.82.

241 Harnecker, Marta, p.89.

242 Pisani, Francis, *Muchachos*, p.40.

243 *Ibidum*, p.38.

244 Weathers, Bynum E., p.43.

245 Harnecker, Marta, p.35.

246 Pisani, Francis, *Muchachos*, pp.118-19.

247 Sierakowski, Robert James, pp.276-80.

248 Weathers, Bynum E., p.43.

249 Pisani, Francis, p.119.

250 William Ramírez, "Unidad construida en la acián" in Baltodano, Monica,, https://memoriasdelaluchaSandinista.org/view_stories.php?id=49

251 Weathers, Bynum E., p. 44.

252 *Ibidem*, p.45.

253 José González and Sandra López, 'El precio elevado de la liberta', in Baltodano, Monica,, https://memoriasdelaluchaSandinista.org/view_stories.php?id=45.

254 *Ibidem.*

255 Myriam Pérez, José Ángel Vindell and Elías Noguera, 'Francisco Rivera entró a Estelí para no salir nunca más', in Baltodano, Monica,, https://memoriasdelaluchaSandinista.org/view_stories.php?id=43.

256 Valdivia, José, 'Qué revolución ni qué nada, lo que queriamos era botar à Somoza !', in Baltodano, Monica,, https://memoriasdelaluchaSandinista.org/view_stories.php?id=69.

257 Weathers, Bynum E., p.45.

258 Orient Bolívar Juárez, 'El Frente sur y la ofensive final del 79', *Bolsa de Noticias*, 23 June, 2014.

259 Bataillon, Gilles, p.188.

260 Harnecker, Marta, p.39.

261 Téllez, Carlos Nuñez, *Un pueblo en armas* (Vanguardia, 1986), p.46.

262 According to the CIA, 80% of the active population was on strike in June 1979, https://www.cia.gov/library/readingroom/document/cia-rdp83b01027r000200030003-0.

263 Harnecker, Marta, p.75.

264 Alonso Porras, 'Los muchachos todo lo hicieron bien', in Baltodano, Monica,, https://memoriasdelaluchaSandinista.org/view_stories.php?id=66.

265 *Ibidem.*

266 *Ibidem.*

267 Mauricio Valenzuela and Danelia Lanzas, 'Había que entrenar, armar y ponerle mando a la gente', in Baltodano, Monica,, https://memoriasdelaluchaSandinista.org/view_stories.php?id=58.

268 Evertz found refuge in Miami, where he died in September 2017 at the age of 91.

269 Myriam Pérez, José Ángel Vindell and Elías Noguera, 'Francisco Rivera entró a Estelí para no salir nunca más', in Baltodano, Monica,, https://memoriasdelaluchaSandinista.org/view_stories.php?id=43.

270 Pisani, Francis, p.120.

271 Javier Pichardo, Cristhian Pichardo, María Lourdes Jirón and Cayando Estelí, 'Somoza salió disparado', in Baltodano, Monica,, https://memoriasdelaluchaSandinista.org/view_stories.php?id=79.

272 Myriam Pérez, José Ángel Vindell and Elías Noguera, 'Francisco Rivera entró a Estelí para no salir nunca más', in Baltodano, Monica,, https://memoriasdelaluchaSandinista.org/view_stories.php?id=43.

273 Pisani, Francis, pp.242-52.

274 Bataillon, Gilles, p.188.

275 Weathers, Bynum E., p.45.

276 Glauco Robelo, 'Pedro Aráuz fue mi maestro', in Baltodano, Monica,, https://memoriasdelaluchaSandinista.org/view_stories.php?id=73.

277 *Ibidem.*

278 Pisani, Francis, *Muchachos*, p.293.

279 *Ibidem*, p.294.

280 Téllez, Carlos Nuñez, pp.54-55.

281 Harnecker, Marta, p.76.

282 *Ibidem*, p.73.

283 *Ibidem*, p.74.

284 Hassan, Moisés,, p.195.

285 Harnecker, Marta, p.90.

286 Téllez, Carlos Nuñez, p.66.

287 Harnecker, Marta, p.81.

288 Téllez, Carlos Nuñez, p.69.

289 Hassan, Moisés,, p.197.

290 Pisani, Francis, *Muchachos*, p.301.

291 Téllez, Carlos Nuñez, p.82.

292 *Ibidem*, pp.86-87.

293 https://nicaraocalli.wordpress.com/2013/07/17/el-ejercito-frente-sur-benjamin-zeledon-y-su-capacidad-de-fuego-en-el-departamento-de-rivas-sergio-espinoza-hernandez/.

294 Valdivia, José, 'Qué revolución ni qué nada, lo que queriamos era botar à Somoza !', in Baltodano, Monica,, https://memoriasdelaluchaSandinista.org/view_stories.php?id=69.

295 https://nicaraocalli.wordpress.com/2015/10/12/toma-de-penas-blanca-en-el-frente-sur-benjamin-zeledon/.

296 José Antonio Molina, 'La macabra masacre de Bélen', in Baltodano, Monica,, https://memoriasdelaluchaSandinista.org/view_stories.php?id=70.

297 Weathers, Bynum E., p.53.

298 Pisani, Francis, *Muchachos*, p.304.

299 Téllez, Carlos Nuñez, pp.97-98.

300 Harnecker, Marta, p.87.

301 Pisani, Francis, *Muchachos*, pp.309-10.

302 Bataillon, Gilles, p.186.

303 Weathers, Bynum E., p.47.

304 Clark, Alexander Bjorn, p.16.

305 Tinelli, Giorgio, p.192.

306 Bataillon, Gilles, p.187.

307 Weathers, Bynum E., p.48.

308 Jaramillo, Jorge F., p.65.

309 Puig, Salvador Martí i, pp.43-44.

310 Bataillon, Gilles, p.187.

311 Weathers, Bynum E., p.49.

312 *Ibidem*, p.50.

313 Bataillon, Gilles, p.189.

314 Téllez, Carlos Nuñez, p.112.

315 *Ibidem*, pp.117-18.

316 *Ibidem*, p.120.

317 Pisani, Francis, p.311.

318 Téllez, Carlos Nuñez, pp.129-30.

319 Hassan, Moisés, p.50.

320 Weathers, Bynum E., p.51.

321 Pisani, Francis, p.283.

322 Téllez, Carlos Nuñez, pp.148-50.

323 Pisani, Francis, p.312.

324 *Ibidem*, p.292.

325 Javier Pichardo, Cristhian Pichardo, María Lourdes Jirón and Cayando Estelí, 'Somoza salió disparado'' in Baltodano, Monica,, https://memoriasdelaluchaSandinista.org/view_stories.php?id=79.

326 Weathers, Bynum E., p.54.

327 Pisani, Francis, p.317.

328 Weathers, Bynum E., p.55.

329 https://nicaraocalli.wordpress.com/2013/07/18/toma-de-la-ciudad-de-rivas-por-la-columna-guerrillera-francisco-gutierrez-sergio-espinoza-hernandez/.

330 Luis Carrión, 'Al final, dejamos las tesis a un lado y nos fuimos a volar verga', in Baltodano, Monica,, https://memoriasdelaluchaSandinista.org/view_stories.php?id=76.

331 Elías Noguera and José Ángel Vindell, 'La toma del Búnker', in Monica Balt Baltodano, Monica,

332 Pisani, Francis, *Muchachos*, pp.334-37.

333 Hassan, Moisés,, p.197.

334 Harnecker, Marta, p.89.

335 Le Blanc, Jörg Heinrich Christopher, p.200.

336 Hassan, Moisés, 2016, p. 191.

337 Sierakowski, Robert James, p. 316.

ACKNOWLEDGMENTS

Projects of this kind are always a matter of lots of networking, and indeed teamwork. The author relied greatly on cooperation with a number of individuals from around the world, who kindly helped collect relevant information and photographs. My gratitude is therefore due to a number of persons, including Mario Overall and Dan Hagedorn from the Latin American Aviation History Society (LAAHS), Pit Weinert, Mark Lepko, Albert Grandolini and Tom Cooper, all of whom have kindly provided advice, additional information and photographs. My special thanks are also due to Michael Schroeder, webmaster of www.SandinoRebellion.com, who selflessly shared the results of his research through the archives of the US Marine Corps and the Department of State. I also thank the entire team of Helion & Company for their remarkable work, without which this book would not be what it is. To conclude, I wish once again to dedicate this book to my daughter Sasha, who gives me the strength and the desire to write.

AUTHOR

David François, from France, earned his PhD in Contemporary History at the University of Burgundy and specialized in studying militant communism, its military history and the relationship between politics and violence in contemporary history. In 2009 he co-authored the *Guide des archives de l'Internationale communiste* published by the French National Archives and the Maison des sciences de l'Homme in Dijon. He regularly contributes articles for various French military history magazines and is also a regular contributor to the French history website *L'autre côté de la colline*.